An Employer's Guide to

Disability Management

Neil Rankin, B.A., A.R.P.

Aurora Professional Press
a division of Canada Law Book Inc.
240 Edward St., Aurora, Ontario, L4G 3S9

© Neil Rankin
Published by Canada Law Book under licence

Printed in Canada

National Library of Canada Cataloguing in Publication Data

Rankin, Neil
  An employer's guide to disability management

Includes index.
ISBN 0-88804-331-7

1. Disability insurance claims — Management.
2. Insurance, Disability.   I. Title.

HD7105.2.R36 2001   658.3'254   C2001-930533-8

This book is dedicated to my family:
my father and mother, Hector and Gloria Rankin;
my brother and sister-in-law, Peter and Louela Rankin;
my sister and brother-in-law, Terry and Greg Hutton.
It is their love and support that have allowed me
to achieve the successes I enjoy today.

Preface

Incredibly, Canadian employers pay 8 to 12% of their payroll on disability claims. That means a company with a $3 million payroll will spend roughly $300,000 annually on employee disability. In fact, one out of seven employees becomes disabled each year. A 45 year old has a one-in-three chance of remaining disabled for more than three months.

Are you at risk? Almost half of today's workforce is made up of baby boomers — many over age 40. The older your employees are, the more prone they are to becoming disabled and then requiring more time off to recuperate.

Despite the enormous costs, most employers take a passive role in ensuring that disabled employees return to work as soon as medically possible. Often, insurance companies and workers' compensation boards do more to manage claims, despite the fact that it is the employer and employee who have the most to gain or lose.

This comprehensive guide will help human resources professionals, benefits administrators, health and safety managers, supervisors, occupational health nurses, occupational therapists, disability management specialists and business owners address their disability management needs.

Among the topics discussed in this book will be: disability management tools, program design, stakeholder responsibilities, returning your disabled employees to work, management principles, modified work and vocational rehabilitation. Also included is a question and answer chapter that may assist during program development.

Introduction

Chances are that if you are reading this book, you may already have an idea how valuable proactive disability management can be in addressing absenteeism, productivity, workers' compensation and insurance costs.

Disability management is much more than simply controlling costs. Employers and employees agree that by implementing a disability management program, workers are happier and more productive, which translates into improved company competitiveness.

So what is disability management? In the broadest sense, disability management is any action that directly or indirectly improves an individual's ability to perform one or more activities. As simple as it sounds, it is amazing how few employers actually apply this to all forms of employee disability. Many employers proudly state that they have a proactive disability management program, and then go on to talk about how proactive they are in disputing claims, calling insurance companies to get a status report or using surveillance specialists to watch unsuspecting disabled employees. These activities are seldom successful in meeting an employee's physical, psychological and emotional needs when returning to work.

This book will challenge some of your current perceptions of disability management while at the same time give you insight into how to develop or improve your program. While reading, I encourage you to take a second look at the assumptions you have made in managing employee disability. You may surprise yourself.

Table of Contents

CHAPTER 1

Disability Management: An Overview

LEARNING OBJECTIVES

By the end of this chapter you should have an understanding of:

- why you need a disability management program
- what disability is
- what impairment is
- the importance of early intervention
- who should be involved in your program
- the importance of ongoing communication, co-operation and consistency

INTRODUCTION

Most employers would agree that proactively managing lost-time claims is a good way to control employee disability costs. The question then becomes, why do some employers who fully endorse this approach experience increased lost-time claim costs? It seems the answer lies in how employers define the term "disability management".

For some employers, disability management is the process of appealing workers' compensation claims or disputing surcharges or simply referring disabled workers to long-term disability insurance providers for monitoring. While these strategies in one way or another have an impact on a company's bottom line, they are rarely successful in returning disabled employees to work and reducing the hard and soft costs associated with employee disability. Conversely, those employers that work in co-operation with their disabled employees, by committing themselves to identifying return-to-work obstacles and taking the steps necessary to facilitate the employees' return to work, reap the benefits. These employers enjoy reduced costs as well as increased profits, by-products of improved employee productivity, customer relations and sales.

What is Disability?

Many associate the term disability with a body part such as the back, shoulder, foot or hand, however, disability really has nothing to do with a body part. Disability is an inability to perform essential activities of daily living, such as lifting, bending, walking, standing, gripping and reaching. Distinguishing between a body part and a disability is critical to the effective management and return to work of your employees. This can be clearly demonstrated by the following case study.

CASE STUDY
Mr. Smith works in the shipping department. He injured his back. He has been absent from work for two weeks on the advice of his doctor. The doctor's note stated that Smith was suffering from a lumbar strain injury and would require two weeks off. There was no further communication between the doctor, the disabled employee or the employer. As a result, it was not determined whether the employee's current abilities matched any of the demands of his job. The employee simply sat at home.

In this case, had the employer taken the time to communicate with the employee and the doctor immediately after the disability, the employee could have potentially returned to modified work on the same day of his injury or shortly thereafter. The point to be taken is that an accident or illness only becomes a disability if and when it prevents someone from performing something they wish to do. In this case, Mr. Smith's back injury only prevented him from performing a portion of his job not the whole job.

Understanding Impairment

It is important to have a good understanding of a person's physical abilities when making a determination on the employee's ability to work, however, this is only part of the assessment. Equally important is ensuring that you have an accurate understanding of your employee's psychological and emotional needs. The importance of assessing all aspects of your employee's needs cannot be overemphasized.

In understanding a disabled worker's psychological and emotional needs it is important to understand the term impairment. An impairment is any loss or abnormality of a psychological (mind), physiological (bones, muscle and organs) or anatomical structure or function.[1] It may be a life-long condition or disease such as schizophrenia or a temporary condition such as a muscle strain that — with appropriate care — will resolve. An impairment does not prevent an individual from performing activities. In the case study, Mr. Smith had lumbar strain impairment, yet he was able to perform some lifting and bending activities. Impairment is most useful in quantifying other potential issues that need to be addressed during the assessment phase. For example, a worker with cancer or post-traumatic stress syndrome may suffer from a plethora of physical, emotional and psychological conditions that require formalized management, while a worker with a less serious disability may only require physical therapy to facilitate a return to work.

It is important to note that regardless of the nature of the impairment an employee will experience, to varying degrees, physical, emotional and psychological distress. The employee may be concerned with permanent disability, risk of re-injury or job loss if unable to resume regular duties. Ultimately, the case manager or co-ordinator and the other stakeholders need to ensure that they have an accurate understanding of each concern to appropriately and efficiently facilitate an early and safe return to work.

Some employers classify employees by disability. They believe that all employees with the same disability should return to work in approximately the same amount of time. Indeed, any employee who exceeds that benchmark is often perceived as lazy or unmotivated. In virtually all cases, the slower-returning employee has additional physical, emotional or psychological issues that need to be addressed to facilitate an early and safe return to work.

---

[1] National Institute for Disability Management and Research, *Disability Management in the Workplace* (1995), at p. 66.

WHY YOU NEED A DISABILITY MANAGEMENT PROGRAM

Invariably employee disability, both at and away from the workplace, costs employers significant amounts of money. For one reason or another most employers fail to recognize the significance of this fact. Listed below are the hard and soft cost areas employers almost invariably must pay for when an employee suffers from a lost-time disability.

Hard Costs

Overtime

One of the most common costs an employer faces after a lost time disability claim is overtime. In this era of company downsizing where employees having to do more with less, most companies simply do not have a reserve list of people with specific skills or abilities to replace a disabled employee at a moment's notice. Overtime becomes virtually inevitable.

With overtime employees are required to fill in for the disabled employee, assuming more responsibilities and more stress. Depending on the length of claim and the number of employees off work, the remaining employees may be overwhelmed by their new responsibilities. This can go on for weeks or months and in some cases can result in new lost-time claims affecting the entire department or plant.

Overtime may work for a few days or even a few weeks, however, getting the employee back to work or replacing the disabled employee must be the priority from both a financial and operations perspective.

Replacement Workers

With a protracted claim — whether due to the seriousness of the disability or lack of proactive case management — the need for a replacement worker grows. Many employers, especially those employing predominantly unskilled labour, believe the quick and easy way to improve production is to hire a replacement worker. It is their belief that by hiring a fully functioning individual to replace the disabled worker they eliminate most or all of the administration that usually accompanies a disability claim: why spend time managing a claim and hoping the disabled employee eventually returns to work, when someone can be hired who requires a day or two of training?

There are essentially three reasons why it is more advantageous to work with your disabled employee rather than seek out a replacement worker. First, if you hire a replacement worker the costs of advertising, screening, interviewing and hiring can be significant. Once the replacement worker is hired another period of time is required to help them assimilate into the job. The replacement worker may have to learn anything from how to operate a machine to the health and safety and general human resources policies of the workplace, not to mention the organizational structure and the particular culture of the new workplace.

Secondly, the costs you incur by hiring a replacement worker may be lost if the reason for the original disability was a result of poor workstation design rather than an employee's inability to work safely. In this case your replacement worker may find himself on disability as well.

Finally, equally significant to the cost issue is employee morale. Have you ever noticed how just one lost-time claim can impact on the morale of many of the non-disabled employee groups? When one or more members of a work team are off work, rapport and synergy always suffer. This is particularly true for both production line and service-related business, where each team member is highly dependent on the other to meet production quotas.

In some instances the replacement worker is considered to be an outsider. Clearly this replacement worker slows productivity due to limited experience and little or no team rapport.

Employers that make an effort to do everything reasonably possible to facilitate commitment to their employees by taking steps to facilitate an early and safe return to work are more likely to enhance employee morale and productivity.

Training Costs

Until someone needs training, you really do not appreciate how technical many of the workplace machines and processes are. For discussion purposes I have divided training into two areas: process training and technical training.

Process training is anything that an employee needs to know to complete one or more job responsibility. This could be delivering paperwork, communicating with a supervisor or reporting an accident. For the most part, this type of training always occurs after the employee has assumed responsibility for a job. It is always company-specific. For example, one employer may have a daily production meeting, while another may have weekly ones. Each employer determines the best process for its particular needs. Therefore, new employees always require an adjustment period to become acquainted with the specific processes of each workplace.

Technical training is usually the primary reason an employer hires a given individual. The employee has certain skills that are required to perform a set of job responsibilities. They have usually learned and perfected these skills over a number of years. While an employer would prefer to hire an employee with a total understanding of a given machine or tool or skill, this is usually not the case. Most new employees require at least some orientation to fully adapt to a new environment.

Whenever a new employee is hired both of these training issues impact employee productivity.

Workers' Compensation Costs and Insurance Premiums

From a cost perspective, workers' compensation and long-term disability insurance are much the same. The more time the provider spends managing or allocating resources to your employees the more the employer pays directly and/or indirectly. To control or minimize insurance costs it is essential that employers assume a proactive or self-reliant approach to managing claims.

An employer can accomplish this goal in two ways:

1. Make a commitment to improving employees' health both at and away from the workplace.
2. When an employee does become disabled, take all reasonable steps to facilitate the employee's return to work.

Remember, the more time off the employee takes, the more money your insurance carrier pays to the employee in benefit cheques. For some employers this can amount to millions of dollars.

Soft Costs

While the hard costs described above are clearly significant, in most cases they are only a fraction of the costs employers incur. Almost invariably, the soft costs shadow the hard costs. Listed below are the two primary soft cost issues that need to be considered.

Reduced Productivity

It goes without saying that when an employee is totally disabled he or she is better off not working. But what about a partially disabled employee, what can you be doing to get him or her productive again?

Most partially disabled employees can resume working within days or weeks of incurring a disability by performing modified work. This happens all too rarely. Many employers avoid bringing employees back to work early for fear of medical complications. Ironically, the care and nurturing the disabled employee requires is considered to be ripe with negative connotations by the employer. It may be the employer's belief that by calling the employee immediately after the disability there is an implication that the employee will not return to work when it is safe to do so. This belief results in lost productivity not to mention the physical, emotional and psychological ramifications the employee experiences by not knowing when or if he or she will be returning. By taking a leadership role in assessing the needs of the disabled employee early on in the process, days, weeks and in some cases months of lost unproductive time can be avoided.

Equally significant in addressing productivity costs are prolonged periods of modified work. Once a disabled employee is brought back to modified work it is crucial that ongoing planning and management (*i.e.*, a return-to-work plan) take place to ensure that the employee moves from performing part-time hours or partial duties to resuming or reintegrating back into most or all of the primary job responsibilities. It is one thing to bring an employee back to work and make temporary allowances for the employee to facilitate their recovery. It is quite another to create workstations that have little or nothing to do with that employee's skills or previous job responsibilities and expect that employee to simply work indefinitely performing what amounts to meaningless work.

Increased Absenteeism

According to Statistics Canada, employee absenteeism is increasing. In 1997, employee absenteeism was 6.2 days lost per worker due to disability and illness, in 1998 it increased to 6.6 days. Even more significant is the increased rate of absenteeism for 55 to 64 year olds. This group's number of days lost due to disability and illness increased from 10.0 days in 1997 to 11.1 days in 1998.[2]

---

[2]   Statistics Canada, Work Absence Rates.

Employee absenteeism can be attributed to a number of variables including work culture, job stress, employer-employee relations and work schedules. By addressing these variables within your organization, costs savings associated with employee absenteeism can be had.

A few years ago, a telecommunications firm estimated that their average employee absenteeism rate was 9.6 days per year. Costs were in the millions of dollars. In addressing this problem they conducted a study that measured employee absenteeism rates for employees during their probationary period and then after their probationary period. Interestingly, they found the average number of days off for probationary employees was three days and that the average number of days for non-probationary employees was 11.5 days, almost four times higher after the period of probation had ended. Chances are good that if you don't have an attendance management program in place at least some of your employees are taking more time off than they need. It is simply accepted practice.[3]

Legislative Obligations

While many employers have realized the benefits of proactively managing employee disability, many have not. As a result, both federal and provincial governments are making it increasingly difficult for the latter group to ignore.

There are two primary areas of legislation that directly influence how employers manage employee disability: human rights and workers' compensation.

Human Rights Legislation

Human rights legislation obligates employers to take all reasonable steps to accommodate the needs of disabled employees. Legally, employers are obligated to accommodate employees to the point of undue hardship. In practical terms, this means that employers must demonstrate that they are unable to accommodate a disabled employee's abilities to a job without enduring significant financial duress. Employers are well advised to consider all possible accommodation avenues prior to declaring undue hardship. Undue hardship sends a clear message to employers that discrimination based on disability is unacceptable. Indeed, it is meant to

---

[3] P.L. Booth, *Employee Absenteeism: Strategies for Promoting an Attendance Oriented Corporate Culture* (Ottawa: Conference Board of Canada, 1993), p. 20.

motivate employers to address employee disability issues internally rather than rely on the courts and tribunals to address these matters. Regulating bodies have sweeping powers including employee reinstatement and financial compensation to address ill-conceived employee disability policy and procedures. The primary consideration when complying with this legislation should be what measures or actions have been taken to demonstrate reasonable accommodation in addressing employee disability on a case-by-case basis.

Consider the case of *Mills v. Via Rail Canada Inc.*[4] Mills worked as a chef for Via Rail beginning in 1970. In March, 1990, he suffered a back injury. Doctors and specialists examined Mills and, finding nothing seriously wrong, Mills returned to work. He re-injured his back six months later and remained off work for six months, finally returning to work on the advice of his own doctor. Via referred Mills to a specialist who rated his impairment at 15% and opined that a return to his chef duties might provoke more back pain.

Via concluded that Mills was unfit for the job and offered him a disability pension but Mills refused, as it was his wish to return to work. The employer then paid for Mills to attend a five-week training course as a telephone agent. Mills completed the course and was offered work out of town, which he refused. Via offered Mills a job in another city and again Mills declined.

In July, 1992, Mills applied for a baggage handler job with Via Rail, however, another specialist deemed him physically unfit to perform the job. Mills complained to the Canadian Human Rights Commission. The arbitrator recommended Mills return to work as a chef with no lost wages. In addition, Mills was to have an absenteeism rate no worse than the average for chefs over the next two years, which Mills interpreted to apply only to time off for back pain.

During the next 15 months, Mills was off work several times for a cut finger, cut leg, burned finger and depression. Via sent Mills a warning letter and in October, 1994, he was fired. Mills complained a second time to the Commission. The Commission found that:

- Mills had been discriminated against as Via had not accommodated his disability to the point of undue hardship;

---

[4]   (1999), 99 C.L.L.C. ¶230-016 (C.H.R.T.).

- Via had not assessed Mills' abilities to perform the baggage handler position, it had relied solely on the doctor's recommendation; and
- Via did not take proper steps to ensure full understanding of Mills' physical abilities.

The Commission ordered Mills to be returned to his chef position with full seniority and that Via pay Mills for lost wages. Mills was to receive interest on his lost wages and Via was to pay Mills the difference in income tax he had to pay on receiving his lost wages. Mills was to receive lost pension benefits and was to be reimbursed for drugs, medical and dental care associated with his benefits. Finally, Mills was awarded $3,000 for hurt feelings and Via was to pay Mills for wages lost in attending the hearings and for travel expenses.

All disabled employees are entitled to accommodation under human rights legislation regardless of how or where the disability occurred. Employers can accommodate disabled employees in a number of ways including:

- providing modified work hours or duties
- investigating productivity aids
- making ergonomic adjustments to the workstation
- re-allocating non-essential job responsibilities
- providing a comparable job that takes into account the employee's wage, skills and education
- developing a transitional work-at-home program

Mills acts as a cautionary tale for employers who shut out their disabled employees. Job accommodation should not be viewed as another piece of legislation that obligates an employer to act, rather it should be viewed as a guiding principle that promotes discussion between the various stakeholders. There is a significant increase in probability of minimizing costs and achieving a solution with which all parties will be happy.

Workers' Compensation Legislation

Workers' compensation legislation developed in the early 1990s as a historical compromise between employees and employers. Employees lost the right to sue employers as a result of workplace accidents, while employers were obligated to pay premiums to offset costs associated with workplace injuries and disease including health care, disability benefits and rehabilitation services. The premiums are used to provide benefits, loss of earnings pensions and rehabilitation (*i.e.*, treatment) for those workers injured on the job.

Each province is responsible for administering and developing workers' compensation legislation. As a result, employer obligations vary from province to province. For example, in British Columbia, Workers' Compensation Board staff manage vocational rehabilitation services. The rehabilitation consultants are responsible for assessing, managing and implementing appropriate programs that will return disabled employees to work.

In Ontario, the *Workplace Safety and Insurance Act, 1997*,[5] obligates *employers* to take a leadership role in returning disabled employees to work. This approach is part of a new self-reliance model the Board implemented in 1998. The Ontario Workplace Safety and Insurance Board no longer employs staff to manage return-to-work programs, rather they view themselves as educators; filling employer needs via training and education for both accident prevention and disability management. This is very much in keeping with the Board's belief that employers should be taking a leadership role in managing employee disability and working with their own disabled employees to ensure they enjoy an early and safe return to work.

Workers' compensation legislation is becoming increasingly onerous for employers. For example, Ontario employers are now obligated by law to contact their disabled workers as soon as possible after an injury and provide suitable employment that is consistent with the worker's physical abilities and earnings. This obligation is designed to bring together the two most significant parties, the employee and the employer to fashion an amicable solution. Despite the obvious benefits of this approach, the new obligations have induced a number of issues that, in many cases, the employer has neither the human resources nor knowledge to manage.

Devoting time and resources to addressing the needs of your employees makes good business sense. Legislation in most provinces is simply an indicator of what the government of the day believes is the minimum an organization should be doing to address a given issue. The most successful organizations in Canada far exceed minimum legislated requirements.

---

[5] S.O. 1997, c. 16, Sch. A.

DEMOGRAPHICS

Simply put, the Canadian workforce is aging. According to Statistics Canada, over half of the workforce will be over 50 years old by 2003. This, coupled with the fact that employees over 50 spend far more time off work due to disability than employees under 50, should be cause for concern for most employers.

According to Andrea D. Trimble Hart, Director of Insurance and Risk Management at Pillsbury Co.:

> More experience may enable older workers to use better judgment in questionable situations, therefore resulting in fewer on-the-job accidents. However, statistics show that the more serious injuries happen to the more experienced workers. "Never quit thinking," says a seasoned worker on an internal corporate safety video. It is easy for a worker to get comfortable, especially after having been in the same job for a long time. That comfort may lead to complacency or inattention, which can cause injuries. Employees with long tenure — say greater than 15 years — may think they know the job so well they can circumvent safety measures or perform the job with their mind wandering somewhere else. They think they can beat the system — and usually they can. However, when these employees do get injured, the accidents can be quite severe . . .
>
> Knowing the demographics of your work force is an excellent starting point to determining if you, as an employer should "think different." How many of your workers are 50 and older? Is your workplace accommodating the various segments of your employee population? If you wish to retain your older workers and keep them safe, you should adjust your loss control program to address age-specific needs related to stress, workplace design and bodily vulnerability.
>
> . . . . .
>
> "As age increases, so does the impact chronic conditions have on a worker's ability to work. Only 1.9 percent of 18-24 year olds are unable to work due to health condition . . . . The rate rises to 18.6 percent for 65-69 year olds."
>
> The arguments in favor of integrated disability management are strengthened by the existence of an aging work force. Streamlined administration creates a more worker-friendly environment for treating any disease or injury, whether occupational or not. A single reporting system for all injuries eliminates confusion about who to call and how much detail to provide.[6]

---

[6] "An Employer's Musings on a Maturing Work Force", *The Journal of Workers' Compensation* (Summer 1999), Vol. 8, No. 4, at pp. 42, 43, 45. Reprinted with

The Importance of Early Intervention

If you do not consider the hard and soft costs, legislative obligations and your aging workforce should be reason enough to implement a disability management program. Consider Figure 1-1. It outlines the probability of a disabled employee returning to work according to the length of time off work. The longer an employee remains off work, the less likely that employee will return to any type of work.

Figure 1-1

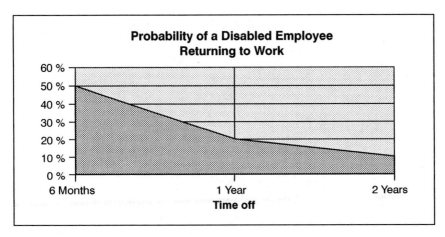

Up until the 1990s, the term "early intervention" was seldom mentioned or used as a strategy for rehabilitating disabled employees. An employee would remain off work until fit to perform all their regular duties full time. Unfortunately, this often resulted in employees being off work for months or years instead of days or weeks. For some their physical, emotional and psychological health deteriorated to the point where they were deemed by funding agencies (workers' compensation boards, government sponsor departments or insurance companies) as totally disabled or unable to perform any occupation. For those unable to work at any job, disability pensions were awarded. These pensions left the disabled individuals dependent on government or insurance benefits for most of their life. The benefit provider placed more emphasis on "paying off" the individual rather than helping to make the individual self-reliant.

Early intervention gained momentum once it was demonstrated that by identifying return-to-work obstacles early on, the probability of returning the worker to work increased significantly, thereby reducing costs. Early intervention significantly reduced the number of workers with psychological and emotional issues — such as chronic pain — thereby increasing the number of employees capable of work.

WHO SHOULD BE INVOLVED IN YOUR DISABILITY MANAGEMENT PROGRAM?

Case Manager or Disability Management Co-ordinator

Critical to the successful management of a disability program is the case manager or disability management co-ordinator. This applies whether you have one or 100 employees off work.

Figuratively speaking, the case manager is the hub of the program. All stakeholders, including the disabled employee, medical practitioners, supervisors, managers and other players associated with a case, report to the manager. This structure ensures that the case manager has a working relationship with all the individuals playing a role in returning an employee to work. This allows the case manager to address and take action on return-to-work obstacles and indeed prevent a return-to-work program from being derailed.

When considering the manager's skills and abilities, it is important to consider all the factors listed below. This list is not exhaustive, every employer will have issues to consider that are specific to their organization.

The first step in appointing a co-ordinator is deciding whether you will have an internal or external one. In most cases an employer with infrequent claim experience will opt for an external manager, while other larger employers with a high claim experience and multiple plants will have an internal co-ordinator. While claim frequency and duration are important considerations, they are not the only issues an employer needs to consider.

The following are some of the issues you should take into account in choosing between an internal or external co-ordinator. Geography, employee demographics and union variables may also need to be considered.

When to use an external co-ordinator:
- no employee currently on staff with skills, knowledge or experience to design, manage and evaluate a disability management program
- total claim costs are less than costs of hiring an internal case manager
- your internal co-ordinator requires outside expertise to reduce claim frequency and duration costs
- you require an individual with an arms-length relationship who will make sound recommendations without regard for organizational politics

When to use an internal co-ordinator:
- one or more staff has the skills, knowledge or experience to design, manage and evaluate a disability management program
- claim frequency and costs exceed case manager expense

No employer with even a single employee off work due to disability should be operating without a case manager or co-ordinator. Using a skilled and knowledgeable manager to proactively manage your cases reduces costs, increases productivity and improves employee morale.

If you are still unsure whether to use an internal or an external case manager, consider meeting an external disability management specialist to evaluate your current needs and make recommendations to that end.

Prior to appointing your case manager, a number of other considerations need to be addressed. Listed below are the essential skills your case manager will need to possess. These skills apply to both internal and external specialists.

Assessment Skills

Managing employee disability is much more than matching abilities to job demands. When an employee is injured at or away from work they suffer physically, emotionally and psychologically. It is therefore important for the case manager to understand how these dynamic variables influence an employee's willingness to participate in your return-to-work initiatives. The case manager needs to understand the disabled employee's priorities. To appropriately achieve this level of understanding, the case manager must have an ability to assess the individual, taking into account all three dynamics (physical, emotional and psychological).

15

Problem Solving

Once the case manager has identified the return-to-work obstacles, an ability to propose and recommend strategies to address the obstacles is essential. Introducing modified work hours or job responsibilities may not be enough to gain approval from all stakeholders. For example, a disabled employee who concludes that his disability is associated with the design of the workstation may oppose a return to work until the workstation itself is modified. In this situation, the case manager would need to balance the rights of the employee with the employer's needs. Likewise an employer who suspects a disabled employee is malingering will need to explore the employee's perceptions, priorities and motivations to ensure everything reasonable is being done to resolve the situation.

Management Skills

There are many management skills required to proactively reduce costs associated with employee disability. Consider the following.

Legislative and policy knowledge

Understanding workers' compensation or human rights legislation simply is not enough to effectively manage a corporate disability management program. Also important is an ability to apply internal employee disability policies and procedures to your short-term and long-term disability ("STD" and "LTD") insurance policies. An understanding of your STD and/or LTD policies is critical to maintaining program cost effectiveness. For example, most LTD insurance policies stipulate an elimination period of three to six months. After the disabled employee has been off for that period of time the insurance carrier begins to assess the employee's needs and in most cases begins to pay the employee benefits. While the elimination period insulates you from frequent premium increases, claims that extend beyond your elimination period can result in significant insurance carrier costs that may result in increased employer premium costs.

By understanding your STD and LTD policies your case manager or disability management committee can ensure all reasonable steps are being taken to eliminate or at least reduce the number of STD and LTD claims.

Counselling skills

Perhaps the single biggest reason employers use rehabilitation professionals (see the Canadian Association of Rehabilitation Professionals

("CARP")) to manage lost-time disability claims is their ability to utilize their counselling skills to safely return disabled employees to work. Unlike many other health practitioners, rehabilitation professionals are trained in counselling theories and practices. They possess an understanding of environmental, cognitive and emotional considerations while serving those in need. Rehabilitation professionals combine their counselling skills with knowledge of physical, mental, developmental, cognitive and emotional disabilities. Information about personal and work adjustment issues, labour market and employment trends, and job placement are also considered.[7]

Successfully returning a disabled employee to work is about relating to the employee's needs on a variety of levels. A case manager's ability to implement counselling techniques will assist in relating to or understanding the many issues your disabled employee is experiencing and in turn will facilitate an early and safe return to work.

Communication skills

It goes without saying that ongoing and open discussion between stakeholders is essential to efficiently return a disabled employee to work. It is quite another matter, however, to say that information being communicated is in fact that which the sender actually intended to say. It is almost inevitable that all or a portion of the information being communicated is lost when two or more individuals share ideas or information. Often this can be attributed to a lack of understanding or insight into the other person's perspective. Employers and employees unable to agree on a return-to-work program often lack the insight required to fully appreciate the others' priorities. If each stakeholder spent just a little time considering the others' priorities and concerns, communication would improve which in turn would eliminate or reduce the amount of unproductive time you and the other stakeholders spend discussing return-to-work obstacles. The case manager's ability to objectively listen to the issues being presented by all stakeholders and then discern which issues actually affect the worker's ability to work cannot be overstated.

Negotiation skills

As a facilitator, the case manager is constantly balancing and prioritizing the needs and goals of all stakeholders. Inherent in this is an

---

[7] Canadian Association of Rehabilitation Professionals, *Practice Guidelines for Rehabilitation Counselors in Ontario* (April 1999), at p. 2.

ability to provide solutions that meet everyone's needs. Clearly, this is never easy. Key to reaching the point where all stakeholders are supporting a return-to-work plan is gaining an understanding of the perceptions, priorities and motivations of each stakeholder. Consider the following case study to assess your negotiation skills.

CASE STUDY

A treating physician informs you that your employee is unable to return to work for six weeks due to a back strain injury. Do you conclude that the employee, in consultation with the doctor, randomly chose six weeks or do you conclude that the doctor is lacking information?

In many cases a physician assessing a disabled employee receives little or no information about the company's policies or procedures concerning return to work. The physician for the most part assumes the worst (no modified work or accommodation measures are available) and recommends to the employee an extended period of time off work. Indeed, the physician's perception, priorities and motivation to return the employee to work are not in line with the employer's needs, resulting in a fragmented situation. Almost immediately the physician and the disabled employee are distanced from a negotiated win-win scenario.

Conversely, when stakeholders are kept abreast of the options, issues and needs of each other, each party has the opportunity to immediately identify common ground and work towards a negotiated settlement where all stakeholders benefit.

Medical management skills

When considering the needs of a disabled employee, it is crucial that the case manager obtain specific knowledge about the employee's medical needs. In most cases this will be obtained from one or more of the stakeholders. While the case manager is not directly responsible for providing medical information, having some insight or medical knowledge concerning the various disabilities your employees commonly experience can be quite valuable in knowing what treatment recommendations or period of absence is reasonable. A case manager should demonstrate a reasonable level of competence in understanding what a physician would consider when endorsing a return to work. This skill will increase the case manager's ability to effectively and efficiently return disabled employees to work regardless of the nature of the disability.

Community resources skills

Any employee off work for more than a week will almost invariably be referred to an external service provider (*i.e.*, physiotherapist) to assist in addressing their return-to-work needs. Just as knowledge and information about medical issues can help a case manager plan an early and safe return to work, having first-hand knowledge about various service providers in your community will ensure your disabled employee is receiving help when needed.

Planning and case load management skills

Managing lost-time claims is an ongoing responsibility for the case manager. This not only applies to the management of the disabled employee but all the other stakeholders. All stakeholders have wants and needs that for the most part can only be realized through case manager intervention. Co-operatively working with all stakeholders will assist the case manager in building relationships that will help to return disabled workers to work. Conversely, the case manager that does not effectively anticipate or plan activities will not only slow the return-to-work process but also alienate other internal and external stakeholders. Indeed, alienated stakeholders focus their time on addressing their own needs without considering the other players. Proactive planning is absolutely essential to efficiently returning disabled employees to work.

In addition to the above-mentioned skills, case managers should also be proficient time managers. This may include efficiently gathering data during meetings or while on the telephone, preparing for meetings in advance, delegating non-essential work, making timely decisions, maintaining accurate case notes and finishing tasks on time. While every case manager has his or her own way of managing time, consider the following suggestions:

- set short and long-term goals
- create a "to do" list every day
- prioritize your tasks
- when reviewing a case, ask yourself, "What can I do today to get this employee back to work?"
- be creative in finding ways to avoid interruptions (*i.e.*, use e-mail rather than telephone)
- say "no" when appropriate

STAKEHOLDERS

While a good case manager is critical to a successful disability management program, there are several other stakeholders who are also integral to the program.

Employee Manager

The employee manager or supervisor provides valuable support in facilitating and monitoring the disabled employee's progress and adherence to the rehabilitation plan.

Disabled Employee

The disabled employee is the source of at least three important pieces of information: identifying return-to-work obstacles; identifying job suitability; and providing feedback about his or her return-to-work plan. The disabled employee has a wealth of information. This stakeholder experiences the process and procedures first-hand. In doing so, the worker can provide feedback as to what works well and what needs to be improved.

The disabled employee, while clearly a key stakeholder in realizing program success, is often left to be a bystander in return-to-work discussions. It is crucial that all stakeholders be viewed as equal partners during all phases of rehabilitation planning.

Medical Doctor

The medical doctor, while a full stakeholder, is often viewed by employers as a threat to successfully returning employees to work. Ironically, employers do not assess or analyze what they are doing or are not doing to address this perceived lack of co-operation. Rather they focus on what they perceive the employee — or the employee and the physician — is doing to sabotage the employer's return-to-work initiatives. When *all* stakeholders fully understand the issues and solutions available to the disabled employee, employer frustration will be addressed and the physician will not be left in the dark about accommodation options.

Benefits Representative

Like the other stakeholders, your benefits representative plays an important role in ensuring your disability management program is a success. Generally speaking, a benefits representative can vary from a workers' compensation adjudicator to a long-term disability or motor vehicle insurance representative. The benefits representative can often make the difference between an employee returning to work or not. Consider the following case study.

> **CASE STUDY**
> Bill has been diagnosed with leukemia. Lacking the resources and the expertise to address his condition, Bill's employer refers him to a long-term disability insurance carrier who confirms that Bill will require surgery, resulting in permanent disability. Following surgery, the surgeon confirms that Bill's cancer was quite confined and that with appropriate rehabilitation he should be capable of returning to work and of performing alternate duties. The benefits representative refers the claim to a vocational rehabilitation specialist to assess Bill's physical abilities, transferable skills, interests and aptitudes. The rehabilitation specialist, in consultation with Bill and the other stakeholders, identifies a job with his pre-disability employer that matches all of Bill's needs. Bill completes a three-month training program and then gradually re-enters the workforce, eventually resuming full-time hours.

Needless to say, without the assistance of the benefits representative, many of the specialty services that were required to return Bill to work may never have materialized. While any qualified disability management specialist could have facilitated this process, it was the insurance company that provided the financial resources that allowed Bill to return to work.

Crucial to the successful resolution of this claim was not only the actions taken by the external service providers but also the employer's ongoing intervention. It is easy for an employer to say an employee is unlikely to return therefore we will not concern ourselves with that. Employers who demonstrate care and concern about their disabled employees throughout the rehabilitation process invariably reap the financial and moral benefits of being an active participant.

Health Care Provider

One or more health care providers may be involved in any one claim depending on the needs of the employee. The most common health care providers are: physiotherapists, psychologists, psychiatrists, orthopedic surgeons, occupational therapists, medical doctors and behavioural therapists. While each provides specialized service in a given area, they all have one common objective: to either restore or maximize your employee's ability to resume their normal daily activities.

In facilitating this process an accurate understanding of the employee's activities is essential. All too often employers do little or nothing to ensure health care providers have detailed information about the employee's pre-disability activities. How can a health care provider assist an employee in returning to work if they don't have an accurate understanding of the employee's job requirements? Health care providers are always pleasantly surprised when they receive a detailed job description including the job title, a general description of the primary job responsibilities and physical demands. Make it a habit of providing this information to the health care providers involved in all your lost-time claims.

Union Representative

The participation and co-operation of the union speaks volumes to both the disabled employee and the organization. By ensuring that the union is a full participant in managing your disability program the comfort level of the employees is enhanced and there is an overall perception that labour and management see eye-to-eye on the importance of maintaining a healthy workforce. It is not enough for the union to simply endorse the program, rather the representatives really must think of themselves as important stakeholders. The union may be able to provide information to assist a particular employee return to work or an idea to improve the overall structure, policies or procedure of the entire program.

THE IMPORTANCE OF ONGOING COMMUNICATION, CO-OPERATION AND CONSISTENCY

If you take and apply one concept from this chapter to your disability management program, apply this. Consistent communication and co-operation with your disabled employees and other stakeholders will always lead to a win-win scenario. This should be applied to all disability claims, whether they were at or away from work (worker compensation, long-term disability or motor vehicle accident). By adopting this approach, employees will have a clear indication of what to expect when they are off work due to disability and employers will enjoy improved employee morale and productivity.

Fundamental to the success of any communication — internal or external — is a set of policies and procedures. The process must be formalized, whether setting up employee contact frequency, program eligibility or external service provider referrals, that way, *all* stakeholders can understand and apply it efficiently.

Some of the most common reasons communication, co-operation or consistency do not occur are listed below. Use Table 1-1 to troubleshoot your program.

Table 1-1

Situation	Possible Solution
• the disabled employee remains off work for an unreasonably long period of time	• designate a case manager with the skills and experience to accurately assess the individual's needs and facilitate a safe and early return to work
• your employee returned to work on modified duties six months ago and has not returned to his regular job	• design a return-to-work plan that outlines the employee's modified work duties, the start and end dates and any other initiatives that need to be addressed to allow the employee to successfully return to his regular job • arrange for a Functional Abilities Evaluation to compare the employee's abilities to the job demands • determine if the restrictions are permanent • obtain the services of a vocational rehabilitation specialist to identify alternate occupations that take into account the employee's pre-disability earnings, skills, interest and abilities

Situation	Possible Solution
• the employee's physician issues vague notes	• have the family physician or an independent health care practitioner complete a functional abilities information sheet that outlines precisely what the employee can do • share job demands information with the physician • refer the disabled employee to an assessment centre for an independent medical examination
• your disabled employee refuses to co-operate with the steps you have taken to return him to work	• meet with the employee to identify the issues • offer more than one option • consult with the other stakeholders to find solutions • write a letter to the employee outlining the provisions that have been made to assist his return to work — include in the letter what you expect the employee to do (refer to company policy and procedures) — include the ramifications of not co-operating • copy the letter to all stakeholders • if non-co-operation continues, write a new letter explaining actions to be taken
• an employee notifies the employer they are ready to return to work	• review your return-to-work policy and procedures • have the employee complete a functional abilities information sheet • contact all stakeholders • ensure job matches employee's abilities • design return-to-work plan • ensure all stakeholders agree to plan

SUMMARY

- Impairment does not always mean disability.
- By thoroughly understanding a disabled worker's physical, emotional and psychological needs, the probability of a successful return to work increases significantly.

- There are a number of hard and soft costs associated with employee disability including: overtime, replacement workers, training, workers' compensation, reduced productivity and increased absenteeism.
- The longer an employee remains off work the less likely he or she will return to any form of work.
- Your internal or external case manager should have community service knowledge as well as assessment, problem solving, management, counselling, communication, negotiation, medical management and planning skills.
- Several stakeholders are required to successfully manage lost-time claims, and include the disabled employee, supervisor, case manager, union representative, medical doctor, treatment providers and insurance representatives.
- Effective two-way communication is key to assessing an individual's return-to-work needs.
- The benefits of focusing on your employee's return-to-work needs far outweigh the benefits of disputing a claim.
- Disability management is an investment in your most valuable asset — your employees.
- You can begin to design and develop a disability management program by appointing a disability management co-ordinator.
- Early intervention significantly increases the probability of your disabled employee returning to work as soon as medically possible
- Today more than ever, employers are buying into the self-reliance model of managing claims

REVIEW QUESTIONS

1. What is the difference between a disability and an impairment?
2. Why is it important to understand your employee's emotional and psychological needs?
3. What legislation governs the management of employee disability?
4. Name six stakeholders that often play a role in managing a lost time claim.

CHAPTER 2

Case Management — The Return-to-Work Process

LEARNING OBJECTIVES

By the end of this chapter you should have an understanding of:

- how to successfully address a disabled employee's physical, emotional and psychological needs
- the three steps to returning an employee to work
- the issues that must be addressed before, during and after a disability assessment
- how and when to arrange a Functional Abilities Evaluation
- how to determine a return-to-work objective
- what to consider before, during and after a return-to-work meeting
- how to use counselling techniques to motivate a disabled employee

INTRODUCTION

No matter how big or small your organization, effective disability management is critical to meeting the needs of your employees and your organization.

The first and most important component to managing a lost-time claim is understanding why your employee is unable to work. Disability is never one-dimensional. An employee with a physical disability has emotional and psychological needs as well. Almost without exception disabled employees feel isolated, frustrated, concerned and anxious about their inability to work. Their source of income and everything they derive from their income is threatened. They may surmise that they are "damaged goods" and in jeopardy of losing their job to a more able individual. Incorporating strategies to address these issues will significantly improve the efficiency of your program.

Most return-to-work programs consist of three phases:

- assessment
- job matching
- case management

This process can be applied to all lost time claims whether they are work related or not.

DISABILITY ASSESSMENT

Understanding your employee's primary return-to-work obstacles requires consideration of a number of variables including the employee's age, disability, pre-existing injuries or disease, length of time off work, treatment needs, educational history, employment history, external stake-holder views and opinions, physical abilities as well as medical, psychological and emotional considerations. All of these variables should be addressed when completing the initial disability assessment.

The disability assessment is usually a one-on-one interview. This approach allows the case manager to understand the individual on many levels. As in any formalized assessment the more thorough you are, the better you will understand workers' needs and the more insight you will gain into the employee's perceptions. This should include their emotional and physical state. As you learn about the employee's priorities relate them to their actions. What activities are they involved with while away from work? Do they suggest the worker is trying to help himself return to work or otherwise?

The assessment interview gives the employee and the case manager the opportunity to achieve a level of rapport that is critical to success. Development of the case manager/employee relationship cannot be under-estimated. Always remember the assessment is not about challenging the worker's perceptions, rather it is a means of collecting important infor-mation.

While the disability assessment can be time consuming, clearly it is a tremendous tool for ensuring that all the information, both positive and negative, is taken into account before proceeding. The assessment phase is a great opportunity to build the rapport that will be required throughout the process. If the employee feels totally comfortable with the case manager the probability of the employee co-operating with the return-to-work plan will improve.

CASE STUDY

Gabriel was employed as a machine operator for a large metal strapping manufacturer. He was unable to perform his job due to a back strain. He had been off work for two weeks on the advice of his family doctor. His employer considered him an average to below average worker. Gabriel was not totally happy with his work situation either.

Notwithstanding this, both parties understood they would have to work together to facilitate a return to work. To accomplish this, Gabriel and his manager met to discuss return-to-work options. The meeting focused entirely on Gabriel's physical abilities. No consideration was given to his emotional or psychological issues. They agreed that some job modification would be necessary to accommodate Gabriel's physical abilities — specifically the lifting, standing, twisting, carrying and bending requirements. The modifications were completed and Gabriel returned to work four hours a day.

Having addressed Gabriel's physical needs, the manager assumed that Gabriel would return to work and begin producing again. A few days later, Gabriel started complaining of pain. While he had agreed to work four hours a day he was actually working half of that. The employer, having invested the time and money into modifying his workstation became frustrated. Gabriel assumed that his lack of production would be used against him and would result in termination. The manager was under pressure to get Gabriel working again to end what some other employees perceived as preferential treatment.

While a number of issues influenced Gabriel's ability to work, the lack of information sharing that occurred at the beginning of the process adversely affected the success of the program. Had the manager had a more detailed discussion with Gabriel at the outset, many of the issues that were preventing Gabriel from adhering to his modified work program would have been addressed.

The more time a case manager spends with the employee talking and understanding the issues, the more motivated and co-operative the employee will feel about returning to work.

No two disability assessments are alike. Indeed, no two individuals are alike. When completing the assessment it is essential that you gather as much information as you can about the employee's perceptions, priorities and motivations. In gathering this information you will begin to understand the factors that will impede the worker's ability to successfully return to work. This process can assist in developing a positive employee/case manager rapport.

Once you have identified the issues, ensure the employee supports your conclusions and recommendations. If the employee's perception is different from yours, additional time will be required to build consensus on the most appropriate return-to-work plan.

CASE STUDY

Mr. Smith was employed as a cable technician. His job responsibilities included running cable, installing cable boxes and testing the strength of the cable signal. The job required prolonged standing, bending, twisting and lifting about 20 pounds.

Mr. Smith injured his back and neck two weeks earlier in a motor vehicle accident. His diagnosis: lumbar (lower back) and cervical (neck) strain. Despite the mild nature of the injury, the worker's physician recommended that he remain off work.

No disability assessment was completed. The employee and the physician assumed the employer would not want him to return until he could perform his regular job. The physician indicated that several weeks of therapy would be required to ensure the employee did not re-injure himself.

Three weeks after the accident, Mr. Smith's supervisor contacted the employee. He questioned the employee's desire to work. Mr. Smith informed his supervisor that he had been advised not to return to work until he had completed several weeks of therapy. Since the company had no written policies or procedures, the supervisor requested a new note confirming when Mr. Smith would be fit for work. This process continued on for some time.

In this case a disability assessment meeting between the employee and employer immediately after the onset of the disability could have been used to educate or reinforce the company's willingness to at least consider modified work opportunities. In most cases, this reduces the duration of the claim. Usually the sooner the employer initiates action on the claim, the sooner the employee returns to work. A number of standardized forms can be used to assist in collecting the information required to implement a plan of action. Some sample forms can be found in the Appendix.

When completing the disability assessment, give the employee some insight as to why you require the information. It will reduce the amount of time required to complete the assessment and give the employee some perspective on what issues need to be considered prior to a return to work. The following paragraphs highlight the major sections of a disability assessment. This information should be obtained as soon as possible after a lost-time claim occurs.

Section 1 — Personal and Claim Information

Make a habit of obtaining the following information whenever a disability assessment is being completed. It will give you a quick overview of the worker's situation and in turn help you determine what additional information is needed.

- name
- claim number
- date of accident or date of loss
- disability
- meeting date
- job title
- hourly earnings
- external and internal contact names
- medication names, dosages and frequency
- pre-existing health conditions and/or disabilities

Section 2 — Review of Medical Documents and/or Functional Abilities Information

This section of the disability assessment should focus on clearly defining what issues or disabilities are preventing the worker from working. This should involve a review of any medical or non-medical documents on file and an open discussion with the worker. Counselling skills can be key to fully developing this section since most employees will report what they believe the employer wants to hear rather than communicate their true feelings. By developing an accurate understanding of the issues the employee will feel more willing to co-operate and participate in the return-to-work process. Listening skills are essential here. You must develop an understanding of the employee's perspective rather than giving the employee your perspective of what they should reasonably be able to do. All stakeholder views are important in the process. The case manager is responsible for ensuring all stakeholder views are considered.

Section 3 — Current Activities

While each worker is different, each employee will adopt a new routine while they are off work. This may include attending therapy, visiting doctors and specialists, performing exercises at home, socializing, searching for a better paying job, participating in academic upgrading, watching television or sleeping more. Depending on the rapport you build with the worker you may be able glean additional information that will help you become more familiar with the individual. Information on hobbies, volunteer work, church activities and family life can help you enhance the relationship you have with the worker and make the worker feel more at ease while sharing information. Any opportunity to build rapport with the worker is worth taking. The more the worker trusts you, the more co-operation you will get.

By learning more about your worker's daily activities you will gain insight into their priorities, physical abilities and interests. This should be used to accurately assess the worker's return-to-work needs rather than to make accusations. Rather than asking the worker why they cannot work, the case manager should be finding out what aspects of the job give the worker difficulty, taking into account the injury, or what steps could be taken to help the return to work.

Building rapport at the assessment stage is crucial. Threats and accusations will significantly reduce or delay a return to work.

Section 4 — Education

This section of the assessment will give you information about skills and abilities the employee may have but does not use on the job. Many employees take jobs that have nothing to do with their skills and education simply because they cannot find a job in their field. If the employee is unable to perform their regular job, you can consider other work that may take advantage of their education or previous work experience.

This information is also useful when it is determined that the disability will permanently prevent the employee from returning to his or her regular occupation.

The section should include level of high school completed and where completed, college or university training, certificates, licences and apprenticeships attempted or completed and the year the grade, degree, certificate or apprenticeship program was completed.

Section 5 — Employment History

If no employment history is available through your human resources department, it is a good idea to gather this information during the disability assessment. There are four primary areas you will need to inquire about: employer details (including location and name), job title, dates employed and job responsibilities. Gather the information in reverse chronological order. The worker's most recent jobs are obviously more important than those done five or more years ago, especially if the job responsibilities were significantly different.

This information ties nicely into the educational information. It further develops the case manager's knowledge of the worker's abilities and can be used to assist in placing a disabled worker into a temporary or permanent alternate job.

Section 6 — Case Manager Impressions

Once you have completed the employee question and answer section, it is a good idea to form some conclusions about how likely a successful return to work will be. By assessing the worker's communication skills, motivation, perceived abilities, job availability, transportation issues, other stakeholder views and opinions, and case manager/disabled worker rapport now, you can begin to develop strategies to address issues that may occur in the future.

Section 7 — Conclusions and Recommendations

This section should compliment the return-to-work plan. It should outline the issues and remedies required to return the worker to work. Just as the return-to-work plan identifies internal and external stakeholder responsibilities, this document should be equally clear concerning who should do what and when. The return-to-work plan may include details about treatment frequency, work hours and duties, specialist appointments, follow-up meeting frequency, internal or external training programs, work trials descriptions, start and stop dates and details on workstation modifications.

This section should also include the rationale for the conclusions and recommendations you have made. Since each assessment will be different, the amount of detail required will also vary. Ultimately, it is the case manager's responsibility to include what is reasonably required to substantiate the recommendations.

The following checklist outlines the information an employer or case manager should consider before, during and after the disability assessment:

Before the disability assessment:
- Provide the employee with any forms or documents needed to determine what will be required to return him to work
- Arrange for the disability assessment meeting ideally before the employee's next scheduled shift or as soon as the employee is medically able to participate
- Advise the other in-house or external stakeholders of the meeting
- Gain an accurate understanding of the physical demands of the employee's job
- Review the employee's personnel file to identify all potential return-to-work barriers
- Review any accident reports and/or other applicable documents
- Determine what information you will need from the employee and other stakeholders during the interview
- Consider what issues the other stakeholders will want addressed

During the assessment:
- Greet the employee and make him feel comfortable, physically and emotionally
- Introduce the other stakeholders and their responsibilities
- Explain the purpose of the meeting to the employee and other stakeholders

- Explain policies, procedures and responsibilities pertaining to the disability process
- Answer any stakeholder questions
- Request and review completed medical and functional abilities information
- Prompt the employee to share his or her thoughts and ideas about return-to-work options to build consensus
- Propose and discuss a return-to-work action plan (*i.e.*, treatment, modified work)
- Write a return-to-work plan with a follow-up meeting date and time
- Review in detail the responsibilities of each stakeholder as outlined on the plan
- Have all the stakeholders sign the plan
- Reinforce the responsibilities outlined on the plan
- Provide the employee with stakeholder contact information (*i.e.*, business cards)
- Always focus on the positive
- Communicate implicitly and explicitly to the employee that it is your intention to work co-operatively in addressing return-to-work obstacles

After the assessment:
- Fax the rehabilitation plan to stakeholders not present (*i.e.*, compensation board adjudicator or insurance adjuster)
- Provide all stakeholders with a copy of the plan
- Encourage ongoing and regular communication between stakeholders
- Contact the employee and the other stakeholders regularly to identify and address ongoing return-to-work obstacles
- Document key issues and facts and address them as soon as possible

Once there is a good understanding of the employee's return-to-work obstacles the case manager, in consultation with the other stakeholders, will need to determine whether the employee is capable of performing his regular job. The job matching process will accomplish this need. Note that depending on the assessed needs of the disabled employee, the job matching and the case management phase may begin immediately after the assessment.

JOB MATCHING AND JOB MATCHING TOOLS

Once the disability assessment has been completed you are ready to match the worker's abilities to a job. This may involve meeting with some or all of the following: supervisor, manager, health and safety representative or union representative. Having a formalized disability management program can aid in ensuring all the necessary players are involved in the process. Gaining the support you need from the other stakeholders is just as important as gaining buy-in from the worker.

When matching the physical abilities of the worker to the physical demands of the job, remember that a disability can have far-reaching ramifications. In other words, it is quite likely that a worker with a back strain will have limitations bending, twisting, sitting, standing, walking, lifting, carrying and climbing. Each job activity usually requires a number of physical demands. For example, driving requires sitting, gripping, bending, pushing, pulling, twisting and reaching. Since each job is unique, it is important to examine the physical requirements of all the essential duties of the job. This approach will ensure no aspect of the job is overlooked. Form 4 of the Appendix is a sample physical demands analysis.

Matching the worker's abilities to a job involves more than comparing abilities to duties, as every individual has his or her own views and opinions. It is therefore essential that the worker be given the opportunity to be an active participant in the matching process. What one person considers to be occasional is repetitive to another. Giving the employee the benefit of the doubt at this stage can make the difference between whether the employee returns to work or whether additional administration is required to work through the issues.

Under ideal circumstances the case manager will have a detailed outline of the employee's physical abilities as provided by either the family doctor, a specialist or another qualified health care practitioner. This information should be detailed enough to allow the case manager to compare the medical information to the demands of the job.

Good reasoning skills are needed to match the employee's abilities to a job. Use several sources of information when determining whether a job is appropriate. Some employees will feel comfortable stating their feelings about the appropriateness of the proposed work. Other employees will rely more on their support network (*i.e.*, family doctor) to determine what the most appropriate action should be. Remember, no two claims or employees are alike, and information gathering can be accomplished in many ways.

Use what seems to address all the stakeholders' needs. Discuss the return-to-work issues openly among all stakeholders. If all the stakeholders view themselves as full partners, probability of success increases significantly.

Functional Abilities Evaluation or Functional Capacity Evaluation

The functional abilities evaluation ("FAE") or functional capacity evaluation ("FCE") is valuable whether your employee has a permanent or temporary disability. Just as a physical demands analysis quantifies the job responsibilities and duties, the FAE quantifies the physical abilities of your employee.

One or more health practitioners, including an occupational therapist, a kinesiologist or a physiotherapist, usually complete this assessment. Depending on the service provider and service request, the assessment may be conducted by a team of specialists. This is called a multi-disciplinary assessment. Virtually any health care provider can be involved. For example, if your employee had a back injury he or she may see an orthopaedic surgeon in addition to a physiotherapist and occupational therapist.

A number of assessment protocols are used in the industry. A protocol refers to the ways and means by which objective information is obtained and reported. While each protocol has its own merits, remember that the main reason for requesting the assessment is to confirm your employee's functional abilities. To this end, it is not unreasonable to request a sample report to gain a better understanding of how the information is obtained and the report is formatted. If you prefer written information, be sure to request that. If you prefer graphs and charts, communicate that to your service provider. Equally important is the methodology used to assess the employee.

Most providers will give you two options, an in-house assessment or a controlled environment assessment. The validity of the in-house assessment is usually quite good. This assessment takes place as much as possible at the employee's workstation. Conversely, the controlled environment assessment evaluates the employee's ability to lift, carry, bend, walk, etc., using weights. The in-house assessment uses tools of the trade (drills, hammers, dies, etc.) to determine the worker's ability to lift, carry, walk and stand. The controlled environment assessment can simulate a number of scenarios, but it will never duplicate a work situation. When matching a worker's abilities to a specific job, the in-house assessment is preferred. If you opt for the less expensive controlled environment assessment, determine if the assessment centre is capable of simulating a workstation. A number of assessment centres use computerized assessment tools to assess the worker's abilities. If the tools used do not approximate the workstation, the actual test result may not be helpful in determining whether the worker is capable of performing the job.

If it is deemed unsafe for the worker to be assessed at his workstation, the controlled environment assessment should be used. The controlled environment assessment is usually less expensive and less accurate in determining if the worker's abilities match the physical demands of a job.

Issues to consider before you request an FAE:
- For what will the assessment be used?
- What questions do you want answered? (*e.g.*, Is the worker physically capable of performing the physical demands of a predefined job? What, if any, additional treatment is required prior to the worker returning to work? What, if any, non-organic impairments are preventing the worker from returning to work?)
- Will the worker participate in a work simulation?
- Is the FAE more than one day?
- What percentage of the assessment consists of the worker actually performing tasks associated with the job?
- What measures have been taken to ensure the evaluator fully understands the physical demands of the job? (The evaluator must have documentation and/or the opportunity to view the job to accurately assess the worker's ability to perform the job)
- What background medical, vocational and psychological information should be shared with the assessor?

Issues to consider when selecting an FAE service provider:
- What experience and qualifications does the assessor have?
- What is the cost?
- Are volume discounts available? (What are the terms?)
- Is the evaluation completed at the treatment centre or at the workplace?
- Is the assessment centre reasonably close to the worker's residence?
- Is the service available in languages other than English?
- Is the report a graphical computer printout or in a narrative style, or both?
- Is the treatment centre an approved evaluation centre used by insurance companies and workers' compensation boards?

- Will the worker be assessed within five days of the referral?
- What protocols are being used to assess the worker: dynamic, static or both?

Issues to consider after the FAE is completed:
- Does the report answer your referral questions?
- Do the testing protocols seem valid and reliable?
- Did the employee co-operate? If not, why?
- What, if any, return-to-work barriers were identified?
- What are the author's recommendations?
- What, if anything, in the report requires clarification by the author?

Physical Demands Analysis

Having a physical demands analysis on hand will speed up the return-to-work process. If you do not have this information available, you will need to rely more on the injured worker's knowledge to determine what aspects of the job he can and cannot do. Seek out other opinions to determine what is and is not essential. If no consensus can be obtained, seek out an external disability management specialist. If this seems to be a re-occurring event, develop a dispute resolution strategy that accommodates all stakeholder concerns. If it is determined that a physical demand analysis is required to return the disabled employee to work, seek out the services of a certified kinesiologist.

Collective Bargaining Agreement Considerations

Increasingly, many companies have disability management provisions written into their collective bargaining agreements. While each company needs to assess their own needs, the following issues should be considered:

- What are the objectives of the disability management program?
- What, if any, impact will the policies and procedures of the disability management program have on other programs, policies and procedures or agreements?
- How will disputes be handled?
- Who is responsible for the administration of the program?

- Who are the internal and external stakeholders and what are their responsibilities?
- How will employee seniority affect work programs for disabled employees?
- What steps will be taken to measure success or failure?
- Is the program consistent with the values of the company?
- Under what circumstances would a disabled worker be eligible for the disability management program?
- What criteria are used to define a suitable job?
- Under what circumstances would the employer modify a workstation to accommodate an employee's disability?

CASE MANAGEMENT

If you are unable to design a return-to-work plan based on the medical information on hand, the case manager will need to take a leadership role to determine what information is required and then obtain it. Generally speaking, if your disabled employee does not perceive the employer as a return-to-work facilitator, the employee's doctor will not either. The better you understand the employee's perspective, the more successful you will be in gaining compliance from the employee's doctor. Always remember to emphasize what you agree on; it will help in addressing the issues in dispute. If the stakeholders believe in the process, you will gain momentum that will assist you in realizing success.

Essential to obtaining stakeholder co-operation from either an internal or an external service provider, such as a family doctor, is ensuring that the service provider has a thorough understanding of all the employee's needs. For example, letting the doctor know about the activities to which the employer is committed (*i.e.*, workstation modification, reduced work hours or duties) can be an important factor in getting the doctor on-side with the program.

Employers often complain about receiving vague doctor notes. Ironically, the note the attending physician provides to the employee is precisely what employers have traditionally asked for. No distinction has been made between absences due to sickness and those due to disability. Indicate to the doctor that you are committed to returning your employee to work. Instead of acting as a gatekeeper, the doctor can then address the medical issues needed to facilitate returning to daily living activities.

A number of tools can be used to help this process. Many employers have developed standardized forms that are provided to their disabled employees whenever the employer surmises that time off may be required. The forms are included in an information package. It explains in detail the policies and procedures, stakeholder responsibilities, return-to-work process and corporate values. The package also contains the information sheets and a cover letter addressed to the physician explaining what information is required and how the information will be used. The cover letter conveys to the physician that the employer is committed to taking all reasonable steps to return the employee to work as soon as medically possible. (See Form 3 of the Appendix for a sample letter.)

If you have been unsuccessful in obtaining the required information from the attending physician, an FAE is an excellent alternative to quantify your employee's abilities. The FAE or FCE, as discussed previously, will outline in detail the employee's physical abilities, such as sitting, standing, bending, lifting, walking and twisting. In addition, the physiotherapist and/or occupational therapist will give an opinion on whether the employee is fit to return to work or not. The report will also include treatment or return-to-work recommendations.

When making the FAE referral, request a "specific" FAE rather than a "non-specific" one. This type of assessment is much more valuable in that it will give you feedback on the employee's ability to perform a specific job. A non-specific FAE will only comment on the employee's abilities. No opinion on the employee's ability to perform a specific job will be included. If you request a specific FAE, the service provider will ask for a detailed job description, including physical demands information. If this is not available, the service provider, in most cases, will visit your workplace to obtain the necessary information for a fee. Most multi-disciplinary treatment centres have the staff and equipment to complete an FAE.

A number of methodologies are used to quantify an employee's physical abilities. When choosing a service provider consider the criteria listed above in the FAE section.

Hierarchy of Objectives

Once the employee's physical abilities information is available, the case manager must determine what job options are available. To complete this process a hierarchy of objectives is used:

1.   Employee's regular job.
2.   Comparable job (within 10% of regular hourly wage, similar job responsibilities, physically appropriate).
3.   Suitable job (lower hourly wage, fewer skills, physically suitable).

Returning to Regular Job

Identifying a job objective is key in determining what activities will be required to return the worker to work. If you are unclear about what job the worker will return to, it is probable that the employee's treatment program is not addressing the needs of your employee. For example, if your disabled employee has a permanent disability and is unable to perform some pre-accident activities, workstation modification or training for a comparable job may be more appropriate than engaging the employee in activities that will be ultimately fruitless. A graduated return-to-work program is not always the most appropriate action plan! Ideally you want your employee to return to his regular job, however, this is not always possible.

Conversely, many employers conclude an employee is incapable of returning to regular duties whether the disability is temporary or not. They conclude that if the employee cannot perform the essential tasks of the job within a few months after the onset of disability, the employee will never be able to perform the job. While a number of factors contribute to employers ruling out the pre-accident job, it is still important for employers to thoroughly assess why they reached this conclusion.

Returning an Employee to a Comparable Job

If the employee is unable to return to regular duties either through a graduated return-to-work program or job modification, comparable jobs should be considered.

A number of variables need to be considered when changing the job objective. Once the decision has been made that the worker's pre-accident job is unsuitable, all return-to-work planning and activities should be focused on returning the worker to a comparable job. This may include on-the-job training or enhancing skills that were seldom used in the past. Physical abilities, earnings, skills and experience, seniority, and employee interests and aptitudes should all be taken into account. This list summarizes the questions you should answer prior to changing objectives:

- Is the employee's disability preventing him from performing the *essential duties* of the job?

42

- Can the *non-essential* aspects of the job be reassigned?
- Would a gradual increase in work hours assist the employee in returning to regular duties?
- Is the employee permanently disabled from performing his or her regular job?
- Will a period of medical treatment restore most or all of the employee's physical abilities?
- Can the workstation be modified or redesigned to accommodate the employee's abilities?
- Has the worker reached maximum medical recovery?

REAP

Comparable jobs are any other jobs that match the employee's physical abilities, approximate pre-injury earnings, work hours, job responsibilities and skills. Ideally, the comparable job should require many of the skills the worker performed prior to the disability. Avoid radically changing a worker's work environment (*i.e.*, construction to office, office to construction). When choosing a comparable job minimize the disruption for the employee; they have enough to think about without having to adapt to an entirely new work environment.

When an employer is unable to match the employee's abilities to the pre-disability job or a comparable job, vocational rehabilitation services may be required. Chapter 3 discusses this in greater detail.

TIP: *Skills checklists for each of your employees are very helpful in determining whether your employee is capable of performing other jobs within your company without expensive training.*

READ ✕ IMPORTANT

Without exception the case manager should never change the return-to-work objective from a regular job to a comparable job until all steps have been taken to rule out the pre-disability job. Once the objective is changed, there is no turning back. A change in objective should never be made if the disability is temporary. Temporary or permanent job modification can always be considered. Ideally, a workstation modification should reduce risk of injury and improve productivity.

Returning to Work with a Suitable Job

If it is determined that no comparable jobs are available, a suitable job will need to be considered. A suitable job is any occupation that fully considers the employee's physical abilities, skills, education, interests and

43

aptitudes. Unlike a comparable job it does not usually approximate the employee's pre-disability wage. Suitable jobs should be considered when it is unlikely an employee will be successful in securing comparable employment. This scenario usually results when the employee has a permanent disability, limited transferable skills or education and little or no training potential. The following case study demonstrates why Mr. Bennett's return-to-work objective was for suitable work.

CASE STUDY

Mr. Bennett is a 56-year-old packer. He permanently injured his right shoulder at work. An FAE recommended that he avoid repetitive forward reaching, lifting, carrying and resistive pushing and pulling. He earned $12 per hour. He has completed Grade 9 and has very limited reading and writing skills. He is not a suitable candidate for formal upgrading. He is unlikely to find a comparable job that takes advantage of his packer skills, as most jobs within this sector require constant reaching, lifting and pushing. His return-to-work objective would therefore be a suitable job that takes advantage of his previous work history and volunteer activities, if any, while at the same time maximizing his physical abilities and earnings potential. In this case a transferable skills analysis would be in order.

Note that when it is determined that your employee will be unable to return to their pre-disability job there are a number of issues that need to be considered above and beyond the factors mentioned here. While it is unlikely that every issue listed below will be achievable, every effort should be made to address as many as possible.

- Where is the job located? (Is it approximately the same distance or within the same city or plant as the employee's pre-disability job?)
- Does the job hold approximately as much prestige as the previous job?
- Does the job, if with the pre-disability employer, have the same seniority as the previous job?
- Does the job give the employee approximately the same amount of autonomy?
- Are the work hours the same as the previous job?
- Does the job offer the same career advancement opportunities?
- Does the new job offer comparable overtime opportunities?
- Does the new job offer comparable training opportunities?

You now have a return-to-work objective that takes into account your employee's physical, emotional and psychological needs. The last step in the return-to-work process is using the medical and vocational information you have obtained to facilitate a return to work.

Return-to-Work Plan

Central to the return-to-work process is the return-to-work plan. The following issues need to be considered when designing the plan.

Stakeholder Buy-in

Working co-operatively with all stakeholders is key to successfully returning a disabled employee to work. While this is often easier said than done, it is important to continuously plan or organize in a way that all the stakeholders support. The case manager needs to understand the politics and the stakeholder personalities. The case manager's ability to understand the issues and concerns of the other stakeholders will assist in achieving buy-in.

The Return-to-Work Meeting

Once you have satisfied yourself that all the components are in place to obtain agreement from each of the stakeholders, the case manager should contact all stakeholders to organize a meeting. Some of the stakeholders, such as a doctor, will be unavailable. This is certainly manageable so long as provisions are made to gain buy-in from them in other ways. At a minimum, the employee, the employee's supervisor and the case manager will need to be in attendance at the return-to-work meeting. Keep in mind that the supervisor will be acting on behalf of the company and will therefore need signing authority to bind the employer to any return-to-work activities being recommended on the return-to-work plan. This usually means agreeing to modify a workstation or paying the employee for the hours worked while on a modified work program.

The following list outlines the issues that should be considered at the return-to-work meeting.

Prior to the meeting:
- Are all stakeholders supporting a return to work?
- Have all the pre-return-to-work issues been addressed (medical treatment, transportation issues, non-compensable needs, training needs)?

- medical and vocational information is available

At the meeting:
- introduce stakeholders and other participants
- explain the purpose of the meeting
- ask stakeholders to confirm information as you present it
- review medical and vocational information provided by other stakeholders
- discuss in detail the issues that may negatively affect the disabled worker's ability to perform the essential duties of the proposed job (visit the workstation if necessary)
- discuss work hours
- if part-time hours are recommended, discuss how the hours will affect the other stakeholders (*i.e.*, production, work teams)
- set a return-to-work objective (see hierarchy of objectives)
- complete return-to-work plan (include job title, rate of pay, activity description, activity start and end dates, cost sharing arrangements if any, stakeholder responsibilities and follow-up meeting dates and frequency)
- review the details of the plan with each stakeholder
- have all stakeholders sign the plan, including family physician
- if the physician is not available, have the employee deliver the plan to the doctor for signature
- set a date and time for a follow-up meeting

Post-meeting tasks:
- fax or mail a copy of the plan to the appropriate insurance agency (*i.e.*, worker compensation board or long-term disability insurance carrier)
- document the information that was shared during the meeting
- notify other departments (payroll or personnel) of the arrangements that have been made
- formally and informally maintain ongoing contact with the disabled employee to provide moral support and encouragement

Once the stakeholders have a verbal agreement concerning what the employee is physically able to do based on qualified medical documentation, and a job has been identified that matches those abilities, a meeting should be arranged between the employee and employer, including the manager, supervisor, union representative and case manager. The meeting should be used to clarify the precise nature of the job responsibilities, the employee's physical abilities and the work hours and start date, as well as to discuss any other logistical issues that affect the return-to-work program. Issues may include a change in shift, a change in work area or work duties, or workstation modifications. The more stakeholders present at the meeting the better. If this is not possible, be careful not to assume what other stakeholders may agree to before writing a return-to-work plan.

During the meeting it is important to convey to the disabled employee that he has a significant role to play in providing feedback to the case manager and other stakeholders and in raising issues. Employees often have the perception that the employer's willingness to even discuss a modified work program is the employer's way of accommodating the employee. They therefore assume that they must extend themselves during the return-to-work program and no other issues are negotiable. The employer and other stakeholders must assure the employee that the modified work program is a means to an end. By working co-operatively, all stakeholders' issues can be addressed.

The return-to-work meeting should be kept upbeat. If you have any reason to think the employee or any other stakeholder will disagree with the return-to-work program, try to address the issues ahead of time. There is nothing worse than meeting without successfully negotiating a return to work that all stakeholders can agree to.

Formulating the Plan

A good return-to-work plan should outline: the stakeholder names, responsibilities and signatures; the return-to-work objective; the activities required to return the employee to work; start and end dates of each activity, and any special instructions such as cost sharing arrangements between two or more parties. Form 1 of the Appendix is a sample return-to-work plan.

Every disabled employee needs a return-to-work plan. There are numerous benefits to taking the time to actually complete this document including: improved communication between stakeholders; consensus between all stakeholders on the best course of action; clearly defined objectives that will help you evaluate your return-to-work initiatives, and an opportunity to build rapport with other stakeholders.

The return-to-work plan is especially helpful when an employee returns to work for part-time hours.

CASE STUDY
Mr. White is currently off work earning $500 weekly in workers' compensation benefits. He and the other stakeholders agree that he is capable of returning to work for four hours a day gradually increasing to eight hours a day. His weekly rate of pay when working full time is $700 a week. His employer agrees to pay the hours he works, a total of $350 a week. The insurance carrier pays the employee the difference between what he receives from his employer ($350) and his disability benefits ($500). This arrangement will continue until the employee returns to work full time.

In this case study, the compensation board would need to know the number of hours and the days the employee is working. The rehabilitation plan will clearly articulate this important information to all stakeholders.

Ensuring you and the other stakeholders have an accurate understanding of the return-to-work objective is absolutely crucial when completing the plan. Return-to-work programs without a plan often result in unfulfilled objectives or employees performing modified work for months or years.

A return-to-work plan can be used for return-to-work programs, vocational rehabilitation and medical treatment, or for other activities that require ongoing review and monitoring. The plan will assist in maintaining communication between all stakeholders while holding the various stakeholders accountable for completing their responsibilities. By developing a plan immediately after the employee loses time, you will ensure all the return-to-work issues are being addressed from the onset.

> **TIP:** *When discussing with a service provider, such as a physiotherapist, the estimated amount of time required to prepare the employee for a return to work, refer to the* Merck Manual[1] *at your local library or bookstore for average healing times. If the therapist suggests a prolonged period of treatment, ask why.*

The Negotiations

Employee disability is more than managing the physical disability, the employee also has several emotional and psychological needs. During the return-to-work phase the employee needs positive reinforcement. This

---

[1] M.H. Beers, R. Berkow, *The Merck Manual of Diagnosis and Therapy*, 17th ed. (Whitehouse Station, N.J.: Merck Research Laboratories, 1999).

includes rewarding the employee for achieving success. This may include agreeing to a return to work, successfully achieving a milestone, reducing medication, complying with treatment schedules or successfully achieving other benchmarks that indicate the employee is gradually returning to his regular pre-disability activities. Get into the habit of providing positive reinforcement on a regular basis. Your employees will appreciate your efforts.

When considering work hours, take into account how much time your employee has been off. In the first instance, ask the employee and other stakeholders for an opinion. If your employee has been off work for more than a week or two, the employee will likely be de-conditioned. In this case the employee will need to gradually restore his fitness level and conditioning. To do this, a gradual increase in work hours will be helpful. Four hours is a commonly used starting point. If in doubt rely on the case manager, as he or she understands all aspects of the claim and is therefore in a good position to assess the needs based on discussions with the other stakeholders.

Once the parameters of the return-to-work program have been determined, establish a follow-up schedule. Ideally, the follow-up meetings should occur weekly until you are reasonably sure the plan will be effective. This should not take more than two weeks. As the employee demonstrates an ability to meet return-to-work responsibilities, meeting frequency can be reduced.

All stakeholders should sign the return-to-work plan. As with any aspect of disability management, stakeholder buy-in is crucial.

The Three C's

Communication, co-operation and commitment are the key elements in all good disability management programs.

Communication

One of the big benefits of appointing an internal or external case manager to manage your claims is their ability to maintain ongoing communication with all the stakeholders throughout the period of disability. So often supervisors or managers are unfairly given the responsibility of managing disabled employees without regard for their many other responsibilities. Not only do the supervisors not have the time to communicate with their employee, they have no time to communicate with the other stakeholders. Managing lost-time claims is always a group effort, if you do not communicate with all the stakeholders, the probability of success will diminish.

Co-operation

Lack of co-operation is often a product of one or more stakeholders not considering the views of one or more of the other stakeholders. Until recently, many employers took the view that if an employee was not capable of performing his or her regular duties the employee would be better off not working at all. This philosophy was rooted in the belief that if a partially disabled employee returned to work, not only would the risk of injury increase but also production would suffer. Employers viewed this as a no-win situation.

Increasingly, employers are realizing that by co-operating with the employee to facilitate an early return to work, all stakeholders benefit. Consider the impact a lost-time claim usually has on a disabled employee:

- you have been off work for a month and you feel useless because you cannot do many of the activities you did before your disability
- you have lost a significant portion of your employment income and are wondering how you will pay your bills
- you call your insurance carrier to ask when your benefits cheque will arrive and they tell you they require more forms
- you are constantly in pain, unable to sleep and have become quite irritable
- you spend most of your time at home unsuccessfully trying to find something to take you mind off your pain
- your spouse and children spend more time asking you when you plan on returning to work than providing emotional support
- your doctor continues to tell you to be patient; recovery is a slow process
- you have no social life as you can no longer play with your children or drive

For most employees even a week off work is a frustrating experience. Any initiatives an employer offers will certainly go a long way in giving the employee at least some hope for the future even if returning to work is not possible in the immediate future. Indeed, by establishing a willingness to co-operate early on, the employee will be far more motivated to return to work, resulting in reduced lost-time claim duration and frequency.

Consistency

Consistently co-operating and communicating with all your employees currently off work due to disability or illness is the third fundamental to proactively managing your lost-time claims. Many employers conclude that if they are successful in applying the three C's to all their workers' compensation claims, they are addressing the problem. Very few employers actually apply the three C's to other (non-occupational) claims. They reason that if they are not obligated to do so by legislation they would rather not commit the time, money and resources.

Ironically, employers who commit the resources required to manage *non*-occupational claims enjoy significantly less hard and soft costs pertaining to employee disability. For these employers it is not a question of whether they are obligated but rather how can they become more competitive and cost efficient. Almost invariably the answer to that question is a healthy workforce.

COMPLEX CASE MANAGEMENT CONSIDERATIONS

While early intervention is the most cost effective way of returning disabled employees to work, it does not follow that those workers off work for several months or years will never work again. The same principles described above still apply. Indeed, employees off work for many months or years often respond very well to the interest their employers show in facilitating their return to work.

When managing long-term claims, more attention needs to be paid to the length of time the employee has been away from work. In addition, emotional and psychological issues tend to be more pronounced. While all these considerations can slow a successful outcome, they may not necessarily prevent an employee from returning to a productive lifestyle. Recognizing the issues and understanding how they affect the employee's needs will give the case manager and the other stakeholders the ability to move towards the desired outcome, albeit at a slower rate.

Keep in mind that every individual will respond differently to activities or recommendations brought forward by the various stakeholders. So long as the activities allow the individual to realize a new level of success, such as improved physical abilities or improved confidence to take on new challenges, this must be regarded as a success. For indeed, without small successes, the large successes rarely come.

> **TIP:** *Rely on the stakeholders most knowledgeable about the claim to identify and resolve complex case management issues. They have the most to gain in the process.*

Counselling Considerations

Incorporating a counselling component into the management of your disabled employees may seem superfluous. However, counselling can have an impact on your disabled employee's ability to focus on the issues that are preventing him or her from working.

Counselling does not always require a psychologist or other professional. The goal is to isolate an issue and develop an action plan to address it. If you determine that the worker or supervisor themselves cannot remedy the issues, use a professional.

The following counselling fundamentals will give you a broad understanding of what is required to successfully develop and maintain a client/counsellor relationship. Indeed, without the presence of any one of these fundamentals the client/counsellor relationship can be lost.

Respect

Communicating mutual respect between the client and counsellor can be achieved in a variety of ways. Acquiring and demonstrating respect by words and actions is essential. Time and time again many employers automatically believe that an employee off work for disability is attempting to get something for nothing. They communicate this through their actions and their words. Rather than identify the issues that need to be addressed, they challenge the legitimacy of a claim, or once a claim is established they challenge every unfavourable decision. What kind of message does this send to the disabled employee, the department, or the company as a whole? In most cases this results in animosity between employee and employer. When the employer finally does realize that it is more advantageous to work co-operatively with the employee it is often too late. The employee has assumed an adversarial attitude toward the employer. Little or no respect exists, resulting in ongoing challenges and a lack of co-operation.

By demonstrating to your employee that you are willing to do everything reasonably possible to co-operatively return them to work, your employee will, in most cases, reciprocate. Some good examples of respect building are:

- encouraging your employee to be an active participant in all phases of the disability management process
- accepting as fact the statements your employee makes about his or her abilities or needs unless proven otherwise
- be non-judgemental about information your employee provides from external service providers

Empowering

One of the most basic human needs is to feel wanted. Empowerment is about communicating to your employees that you believe they have a number of valuable skills that can be used to address an issue whether that issue is away from or at work. It is not enough for an employer to say so, the employee must be made responsible for matters in which he or she has competence. For example, in the case of a lost-time claim, it is rare that the employee is asked for input into the possible return-to-work options. In most cases, the employee sits passively waiting to be told what to do and when to do it. The employee should be encouraged to contribute to solving return-to-work issues as a full participant. Some companies encourage employees to analyze their workstations to recommend changes to improve efficiency and productivity. There is no reason why a similar arrangement could not occur in bringing a disabled employee back to work.

Educating

Helping employees understand the issues that directly influence their beliefs and motivation can make a significant difference in hastening an early and safe return to work.

Take, for example, the case of soft tissue injuries. When employees feel pain they generally stop what they doing. They reason that the pain indicates something unhealthy. However, in this case — after addressing muscle inflammation — muscle movement and reactivation should be *encouraged*. In this case, pain is part of the process of re-conditioning the muscles to regain the strength and endurance enjoyed prior to the impairment. Clearly, by educating employees about this they become more in control and in turn adapt to the new information.

Educating employees can be as simple as providing information sheets or articles about common myths or misconceptions about various injuries that are taken for granted.

Informed Decision-making

As a case manager you are charged with laying out the various options your employee may choose to act on. Counselling is not about making decisions. By providing the information the employee requires to make an informed decision, you can be reasonably assured that the client will accept the recommendation, therefore increasing the chances of success.

When laying out the options, use your experience to share issues that the less knowledgeable client would not think of. Providing this insight allows the worker to make an informed well-thought-out decision.

Confidentiality

It is one thing to discuss a lost-time claim generally and generically with colleagues or friends to gain perspective or a second opinion on a given issue; it is quite another to discuss or access employee medical information without first obtaining consent from the employee. Generally speaking, the *only* time specific claim information (*e.g.*, the employee's name, medical conditions, claim numbers, written documentation) should be provided is for the purposes of improving the employee's return-to-work potential. This may include any type of disability assessment, treatment or return-to-work initiatives.

The following elements should be included on the release form:

- worker's name
- reason information is required
- length of time release is valid (*i.e.*, one year or length of claim)
- witness line for signature
- document date

Competence

You may possess all the attributes to be a great case manager, but if you are not perceived as competent by your employee, it will be very difficult to gain the confidence you will require to perform your responsibilities.

Gaining the level of competence required to address your client's needs is not so much what you say, but what you do. A client is more likely to regard you as a competent practitioner when you demonstrate an ability to provide insight into issues that the client could not otherwise deduce on his or her own. The manager must feel competent in their abilities to address the issues at hand. If this is not the case, alternatives need to be considered and pursued.

Ethics

Ethics are a set of rules and practices usually associated with a given profession. While each profession has tailored their statements to their profession, many ethical issues are shared regardless of profession. The Canadian Association of Rehabilitation Professionals provided the following:[2]

Code of Ethics and Standards

Section A: Moral and Legal Standards
[Rehabilitation counsellors] will behave in a legal, ethical and moral manner in the conduct of their profession, maintaining the integrity of the Standards and avoiding any behaviour, which would cause harm to others.

. . . . .

Section B: Member-Client Relationship
Members shall respect the integrity and protect the welfare of people and groups with whom they work. The primary obligation of the member is to their clients and they shall endeavour at all times to place their clients' interest above their own. Members will make clear to clients the purposes, goals, and limitations that may affect their relationship.

. . . . .

Section C: Advocacy
Members shall serve as advocates for people with disabilities.

. . . . .

Section D: Professional Relationships
Members shall act with integrity in their relationships with colleagues, other organizations, agencies, institutions, referral sources, and other professions to facilitate the contributions of all specialists toward achieving optimum benefits for clients and promoting advancement within the field of rehabilitation.

. . . . .

---

[2] CARP Code of Ethics and Standards (approved: CARP National AGM, October 1995), taken from the Canadian Association of Rehabilitation Professionals website: www.carpnationional.org. Reprinted with permission.

Section E: Professional Business Practices

Members shall adhere to professional standards in establishing fees and marketing their services.

. . . . .

Section F: Confidentiality

The member has a duty to hold in confidence all information concerning the affairs of the client acquired in the course of the professional relationship and should not divulge such information.

. . . . .

Section G: Assessment

Members shall promote the welfare of clients in any of the following assessment related activities: selection, utilization and interpretation of assessment measures as well as the implementation of recommendations.

. . . . .

Section H: Research Activities

Members shall assist in efforts to expand the knowledge needed to more effectively serve people with disabilities.

. . . . .

Section I: Competence

Members shall establish and maintain their role competencies at such a level that their clients receive the benefit of the highest quality of service.

. . . . .

Section J: Registration/Accreditation

Members holding the RRP/ARP designation shall honour the integrity and respect the limitations placed upon its use. (Note: Name of the designation changed effective January 2000.)

Section K: Conflict of Interest

Members will ensure there is full disclosure to all parties should their ancillary interest be seen as a real or perceived conflict of interest.

. . . . .

Section L: Service Delivery

Members shall deliver and document services in a timely, objective and comprehensive manner, appropriate to the members' role.

Conflict of Interest

Conflict of interest results when one or more stakeholders are misled or not informed about a third party relationship that may jeopardize the relationship between one or more of the stakeholders. This should be addressed in the company's policy and procedure manual. The procedures should clearly articulate the information that needs to be disclosed including why a conflict situation may exist, to whom the information should be provided and when.

A number of organizations and associations have very detailed conflict of interest protocols that can be used to assist an employer in developing their own policy and procedures.

SUMMARY

- Assess your disabled employee's needs from a physical, emotional and psychological perspective.
- Establish rapport with the employee by demonstrating an ability to understand the issues he or she is experiencing.
- No two employees are alike. Assess each employee based on the issues, not on impairment.
- Always work towards gaining buy-in from all stakeholders.
- Early intervention means assessing need immediately after the employee becomes disabled.
- The disability assessment should include medical and functional abilities information, worker's current activities, level of education, employment history, case manager impressions and an action plan.
- An FAE will clearly articulate what the worker is physically capable of doing.
- A physical demands analysis should be used to quantify the essential duties of a job.
- The case manager is the hub of all disability management activities.
- Communication, co-operation and consistency are key to managing claims.
- Use the hierarchy of objectives to help determine what issues need to be addressed in the return-to-work plan.

REVIEW QUESTIONS

- Under what circumstances should an FAE be used?
- Why is stakeholder buy-in important?
- What are the three C's of effective disability management?

CHAPTER 3

Vocational Rehabilitation

LEARNING OBJECTIVES

By the end of this chapter you should have an understanding of:

- the definition of vocational rehabilitation
- how to determine when vocational rehabilitation activities are necessary
- how to apply the vocational rehabilitation process to your employee
- how to match a suitable job to the employee's abilities
- how and when to use external service providers
- how to assess employability
- essential elements of a transferable skills analysis
- how and when to use vocational rehabilitation tools
- how to address the psychological issues associated with permanent disability

INTRODUCTION

Vocational rehabilitation is the process of matching an employee's physical abilities, skills, knowledge, aptitudes, interests, training and experiences to an occupation. Vocational rehabilitation consists of four phases: assessment, research, job preparation and implementation.

Assessment may include one or more of the following: transferable skills analysis, vocational evaluation and psycho-vocational evaluation. These three assessment tools while unique, all fundamentally assist the case manager in identifying possible job options that take into account the employee's skills and experiences.

Once a number of occupations have been identified that appear to be appropriate, the case manager or designate, along with the disabled employee, identify the various other considerations that will be important in determining which occupations will be best suited to the employee's needs. Research may include talking to individuals who are knowledgeable about a given field or sector, accessing reference guides (*i.e.*, *National Occupational Classification*[1]), books and manuals to confirm availability of work in a given region, and gaining detailed wage and physical abilities information (*e.g.*, we may know that a inventory clerk stands but do they stand 20%, 50% or 80% of their shift?). Research will provide the stakeholders with the information required to determine if a job is appropriate and if any training is required to perform the job. Gaining information about a given job is essential to ensure that the job is suitable and that all issues pertaining to the skills and knowledge required to perform the job are accounted for. In keeping with this theme, it is important to involve the disabled employee as much as possible in the research phase. The more time the employee spends researching, the more understanding and confidence they will have in acquiring the skills and actively seeking out work. Research that you assign to the employee will vary depending on the employee's abilities. If the employee lacks the skills to research independently, the case manager should make an effort to work with the employee in directing his or her research activities. All stakeholders will benefit.

Before moving into the job preparation phase, you should have at least three job options that you feel reasonably match the employee's physical abilities, pre-existing skills, aptitudes, interests and experiences. Of those three jobs, one should be chosen as the preferred job option based on the employee's interests, associated costs, potential for eliminating wage loss and working conditions.

If, during the research phase, it is determined that the employee will require additional skills to successfully compete for the preferred job, you will need to be very specific about what upgrading requirements the employee will require. For example, if, through a psycho-vocational assessment, the employee has demonstrated an ability to successfully complete post-secondary training but lacks the prerequisite training to gain admission, admission testing and/or high school education upgrading will

---

[1]   (Ottawa: Employment and Immigration Canada, 1993).

need to be factored into the plan. If the employee requires significant pre-admission upgrading, this job option may be inappropriate. These types of decisions should take into consideration the short and long-term benefits such as: probability of success during and after program completion; job suitability; and job availability immediately after program completion and in the future. The job preparation phase may be a few weeks, months or more depending on the employee's needs.

> **TIP**: *If you are considering a long job preparation phase for your employee, be sure the recommended action plan restores at least 90% of the employee's pre-disability earnings. The more time you and the disabled employee spend preparing for job re-entry, the more expensive the plan will become. To offset the preparation costs there should be little or no wage loss following completion of the program.*

Once you have narrowed down the number of occupations that appear to be well-suited to the employee's skills and abilities, a formal return-to-work plan is organized in consultation with the employee and the other stakeholders. This is the implementation phase. The return-to-work plan should outline precisely what is required to facilitate a return-to-work (*i.e.*, academic upgrading, on-the-job training, job searching, English upgrading, equivalency testing, skills training, work hardening, work trial or a transitional work program). The research information you gathered will assist you in details such as start dates and costs required to ensure the employee successfully completes the plan.

In most cases, the disabled employee is unfamiliar with the vocational rehabilitation process. It will therefore be necessary to address the issues and concerns with which the employee will undoubtedly seek assistance. This aspect of the vocational rehabilitation process is significant. By ensuring the employee is at ease and comfortable with the process, you will increase the probability of the employee's success. Addressing the employee's needs and ensuring he or she is at ease throughout the vocational rehabilitation process is the responsibility of the case manager.

As you can see, vocational rehabilitation activities can be quite time-consuming. For this reason it is helpful to consider job options that will allow the employee to re-enter the labour force with little or no formal upgrading. Indeed, costs associated with workstation modifications can amount to only a fraction of the costs you may incur by initiating the vocational rehabilitation process. It is better to have considered direct entry job options and discover that they are not appropriate than not to have considered them at all.

In addition to matching the employee's skills and abilities to a physically appropriate job, a number of other considerations must also be addressed. These issues are discussed at length below. The phases listed below apply to all individuals participating in a vocational rehabilitation program.

Note that the above section provides an overview of the phases associated with effective vocational rehabilitation services. It is not meant to be exhaustive, as in most cases professional case management firms are required to facilitate the process. Usually employers have neither the time nor the expertise to manage these types of claims. By referring the case to an external service provider, all the issues can be fully considered by experienced vocational rehabilitation professionals.

IS VOCATIONAL REHABILITATION NECESSARY?

The questions in Table 3-1 should be considered prior to commencing a vocational rehabilitation plan:

Table 3-1

Instructions: Answer yes or no to the following. If you answer yes to all or most of the questions listed below, the employee is a suitable candidate for vocational rehabilitation services.		
Medical Considerations	Yes	No
Is the employee permanently disabled?		
Has the employee reached maximum medical recovery?		
Does the disability prevent the employee from performing the essential duties of the pre-disability job or a comparable job?		
Employability Considerations		
Is it reasonable to conclude that the employee will be capable of returning to work in any occupation?		
Does the employee need direction in identifying an alternate job?		
Is the employee retiring within the next two years?		

	Yes	No
Psycho/Social Considerations		
Is the employee motivated to return to work?		
Is the employee emotionally and psychologically capable of participating in the vocational rehabilitation process?		
Has the employee learned to manage pain?		
Financial Considerations		
Are the compensation board, insurance provider or other providers willing to sponsor the costs associated with the vocational rehabilitation program?		
Is it cost effective for the employer to fund a vocational rehabilitation program?		
By implementing the vocational rehabilitation program is it reasonable to conclude that the employee will be successful in returning to full-time work?		

APPLICATION

Once it has been determined that the employee would benefit from vocational rehabilitation services, appropriate assessment will be required to ensure that all the employee's needs are taken into account. Issues may include financial concerns, employability issues (*i.e.*, ability to work full-time hours) and job search issues.

The assessment will ensure all these issues are taken into account prior to preparing a vocational rehabilitation action plan. With that in mind, it is crucial that an appropriate assessment be completed to ensure the plan meets the needs of all the stakeholders.

Assessment

An accurate individualized assessment is crucial to achieving a successful outcome. In most cases the assessment phase begins by identifying an employee's transferable skills. The transferable skills analysis identifies: the employee's skills, abilities and experiences by gaining a detailed understanding of the disability; work history (including job title, location, wage, work hours, duties, required skills and reason for leaving); and personal history (including date of birth, country of origin, marital status, dependants, languages spoken and benefit entitlement). It also examines the employee's formal qualifications such as licences and designations associated with training or experience.

An analysis of the employee's skills should not be limited to paid employment. Volunteer work, hobbies and participation in community activities all enhance an individual's marketability. The more skills an employee has, the more success he or she will have in becoming reintegrated into the workforce.

TIP: *When gathering information about the employee's activities, attempt to draw out the topics and activities in which the employee seems most interested. These will assist in identifying activities about which the employee will get excited and motivated.*

During the assessment phase of the process the employee will require ongoing encouragement and support to cope with the issues that require attention. This should be monitored on an ongoing basis.

On occasion the transferable skills analysis will not provide you with all the information you require to appropriately match the employee's skills to a new job. The employee may require one or more additional assessments to appropriately determine what job options will best suit the employee's skills, physical abilities, learning potential and pre-disability wage. Listed below are the most common scenarios that require additional assessment. If these points apply to your employee, a vocational or psycho-vocational assessment may be in order:[2]

- the employee was a medium to high wage earner with only a few transferable skills
- it is unlikely the employee will be successful in returning to alternate work using his or her current skills
- six months or more of upgrading is required to restore the pre-disability income
- it is unknown if the employee has the cognitive abilities required to upgrade his or her skills
- the employee may experience difficulty coping emotionally or behaviourally to vocational rehabilitation activities

---

[2] Table 3-2 gives further information on assessments beyond the transferable skills analysis.

Vocational or psycho-vocational assessments should be completed by one or more qualified vocational professionals. They have the expertise to quantify the information required to identify alternate occupations. Indeed they will minimize the disruption the employee is experiencing as a result of the disability.

Matching a Job to the Employee

As previously mentioned, it is very important to identify activities that the employee enjoys. The more focus you place on activities the employee enjoys, the greater the likelihood of finding a job that he or she will be interested in pursuing.

The points below identify a number of job suitability issues. Once a few job options have been identified, use these points to fully assess the suitability of the identified job options.

Level 1
- Does the job match the worker's physical abilities?
- Is the job available in the employee's community or within reasonable commuting distance?
- Do the job requirements take advantage of the employee's education, training and skills?
- Does the job maximize the employee's earnings potential, taking into consideration physical abilities and job opportunities in the community?

Level 2
- Is it reasonable to conclude the worker will be able to secure employment in this field following completion of the labour market re-entry plan?
- Is it reasonable to conclude that the employee will be successful in completing any formalized or informal training required to compete for the job?
- Will the job be in demand five years from today?
- Is the pay range similar to the employee's pre-disability pay range now and in the future?
- Does the job offer similar promotion opportunities?
- Does the job offer similar prestige?
- Does the job offer a similar quality of life (*i.e.*, hours of work, amount of travel required)?

- Does the employee have the aptitudes required to satisfy all aspects of the job?

A number of variables beyond the issues mentioned above need to be considered in determining if a job is suitable. In most cases a disabled employee has a lot to consider when faced with the reality that he or she will not be returning to their regular job. Issues such as work environment, adapting to new people and responsibilities, and building confidence in their ability to secure new work all influence the employee's ability to successfully adapt to a new job.

For these reasons the employee should be an active player, whether that may be participating in a skills analysis or conducting labour market research. Motivation is directly proportional to buy-in, the more buy-in the employee and other stakeholders have, the more motivated they will be to realize a successful outcome.

Formal Training

In some instances a disabled employee requires training to ensure they have the skills necessary to restore all or the majority of the pre-disability income. Training can vary from a one-day computer course to one or more years of technical training.

There are a number of assessment tools available to confirm an employee's suitability for formal training. Table 3-2 summarizes the assessment tools used by vocational rehabilitation practitioners; use it to help determine when a specific assessment should be used.

Table 3-2

Issue to be addressed	Recommended Assessment
Is the job within the employee's physical abilities?	Functional abilities evaluation
Does the employee have the learning potential, skills and aptitudes required to complete formalized training?	Vocational assessment
Is the employee demonstrating psychological dysfunction?	Psychological assessment

Issue to be addressed	Recommended Assessment
Is the employee demonstrating psychological dysfunction and does he or she require training to re-enter the workforce to approximate their pre-disability earnings?	Psycho-vocational assessment
Is the employee employable?	Controlled situational assessment
What job options — taking into account work experiences, earnings, physical abilities, education, interests, aptitudes and labour market — are suitable?	Vocational assessment

When requesting one or more of these assessments, it is imperative that the referrer outline specifically what issues need to be answered prior to completing the assessment. By using the "Issues" column you can articulate to the service provider precisely what questions you want answered.

TIP: *It is not in your interest or the employee's interest to request specific tests (i.e., aptitude, interest and intelligence). The evaluator is much more knowledgeable about what tests will address your referral questions. Ask the questions and allow the evaluator to determine the best way to answer your questions.*

Issues for consideration before training:
• Does the employee have the interest or aptitudes required to successfully complete the training program?
• Will the training ensure the employee is able to approximate his or her pre-disability income?
• Is it reasonable to conclude that the employee's new skills will be in demand following completion of the training?
• Are the skills in demand in your employee's community?
• Does the training institution offer job placement services and what is its success rate for placing students after graduation?
• Does the training include work placements (paid or otherwise)?
• Does the training institution have a track record or specialized services that serve the needs of the employee better than other training institutions?

- Is the training centre located in close proximity to the employee's residence?

Issues for consideration during training:
- Is the employee successfully completing work assignments, tests and exams?
- What, if any, issues may prevent the employee from successfully completing the training?
- What can be done to address the issues?

Issues for consideration after training:
- Has the employee satisfied licensing (*e.g.*, forklift licence) and/or graduation requirements to be considered employable?
- Does the employee have the job search skills required to secure a job in his or her new field?

EXTERNAL SERVICE PROVIDERS

Just as a good disability management program relies on a number of specialty service providers to successfully manage claims, so do vocational rehabilitation specialists rely on service providers to effectively return a disabled employee to work. External service providers have the necessary skills, abilities and resources required to efficiently address needs in a timely fashion. The provider will give you an objective assessment of one or more issues that can be used to further the return-to-work process.

Inherent in the specialization of services is the fact that no one provider can satisfy all your needs. As tempting as it may be, do not assume one provider, despite their claims, can provide you with all the answers. Verify the information they provide by contacting other providers. By comparing the information you gain, you will be in a better position to select the most appropriate provider.

The list below outlines some hints for selecting a provider. These considerations apply to virtually every service provider, whether related to vocational rehabilitation or not. More detailed information about service providers can be found in Chapter 5.

When selecting an external service provider:

- get detailed information about when and where the assessment will be done, who will complete the assessment and the cost
- call the assessor to communicate the issues as you see them
- determine what experience the provider has in providing the service you are requesting
- ask colleagues or friends about service providers they use
- *do not* ask the service provider to do something beyond their service capabilities
- *do not* expect the service provider to understand the issues pertaining to the claim unless you discuss the issues with them
- *do not* refer to a service provider until you have considered all the possible outcomes

ASSESSING EMPLOYABILITY

Assessing the employability of your employee is no different than many of the other issues that have been discussed. It should always be individualized. You cannot make assumptions based on the employee's disability or job requirements. Every employee is different; every disability is unique to the individual.

If the employee has been off work a long time, it is recommended that a disability management specialist be used to assess the employee's ability to work. The sections discussed below provide an overview of the issues that need to be considered. Depending on the needs of your employee, one or more additional services may be required to confirm employability.

Physical Considerations

While the primary reason for an employee being off work may relate to a workplace accident, this does not preclude other disabilities or impairments from affecting the employee's ability to work. It is one thing to conclude that an employee is fit to work based on the issues identified on the original claim, it is quite another to return an employee to work without regard for other non-compensable issues.

Always take the time to consider the employee as a whole rather than focusing on a body part. The employee's overall health should always be the main priority whether or not there is one or more unrelated return-to-work obstacle. Employers should work with their disabled employees based on their ability to identify a suitable job, not based on the origin of the disability. If the employer is unable to identify suitable work for the employee — taking into account their physical abilities, wage and skills — external service providers, such as long-term disability or the workers' compensation board, should be involved.

Performance Considerations

Productivity is always a concern especially when an employee has been off work for a prolonged period of time (three months or more). Productivity differentiates between what an employee can physically do and what he or she can productively do. This is an important distinction. In today's competitive work environment it is not appropriate to simply give a disabled employee a job to demonstrate good will. This not only insults the employee and their co-workers, but it also makes no business sense. Who would hire someone who can produce 100 widgets a day when the company needs 200 widgets a day to be competitive?

There should be no long-term productivity allowances made for a disabled employee. Productivity allowances should be used as a means of facilitating a graduated early and safe return to work. If the stakeholders reach a consensus on return-to-work parameters, clear timelines need to be established before the graduated return to work begins. If after a reasonable period of time the employee is unable to demonstrate an acceptable level of productivity and hours, the employee should be re-evaluated physically, emotionally, behaviourally and psychologically.

In assessing your employee's ability to perform the essential duties of a job, you may want to consider using external service providers. External providers can offer a wide range of services to better assess the employee. This in turn will ensure that you obtain the information you require to make a sound decision. For example, a controlled work assessment centre can assess the employee's ability to perform a given job by measuring his or her ability to perform a given set of tasks. More information on controlled assessments can be found in Chapter 5.

Punctuality and Attendance

It goes without saying that a disabled employee who is unable to physically, emotionally or psychologically attend work on a daily basis is unlikely to be deemed employable. Having said that, it is important to understand that there may be other issues that may be viewed by one or more of the stakeholders as return-to-work obstacles. They may include transportation issues, treatment sessions or daycare. This is particularly true for employees who have been off work for an extended period of time. They quickly develop new routines that suit their new lifestyle. In most cases these types of issues can be resolved by open dialogue with the stakeholders. For example, in the case of treatment sessions, it should be explained to the employee that the conditioning that he or she has received via therapy will be replaced by attending work on a daily basis. In this situation, therapy frequency may be reduced and arranged around the employee's graduated return-to-work hours.

Employee Learning Abilities

One of the big advantages of returning an employee to work with the pre-disability employer is the familiarity both the employer and the employee have for each other. This is quite helpful in effectively managing the employee's return-to-work needs. The more familiar you are with your employee's learning style, skills and aptitudes, the more apt you will be in matching the employee to a suitable job. This information can also be helpful in determining if the employee is a suitable candidate for formal retraining. If the employee has not demonstrated an ability to learn in a classroom setting in the past, formalized testing should be completed prior to considering a formal training program.

Psycho-Social Considerations

When an employee is unable to return to his or her pre-disability occupation, they may experience a period of withdrawal that can extend well beyond the primary return-to-work issues. They may experience periods of denial, anger, isolation and depression both from a job perspective and a personal/family perspective. All these issues can affect the employee's ability to regain many of the activities of daily living they enjoyed previously. Depending on the severity of these considerations, an employee may be advised by a treatment provider to abstain from working until their issues have been addressed. While every case is different, using a graduated approach — whereby the employee is brought back to work performing just a few of the activities he or she will be expected to perform full time — is an excellent method to build the confidence the employee will need to regain most of his or her pre-disability activities. In many instances the employee can start working at home in preparation for re-entering the regular workforce.

CASE STUDY
Martha was a dietitian for a large nursing home. She had a long history of psychological dysfunction relating to stress and phobias. Following a two-year period of absence from her pre-disability job it was determined that another less stressful occupation might be in order. Various assessments were completed. Following the assessments, Martha was concerned about how she would be perceived by her co-workers, not to mention the impact the new job would have on her own psyche.
Recognizing Martha's concerns, her pre-disability employer provided her with work that would facilitate a gradual increase in responsibilities. She worked from home for several weeks performing computer-based activities. She traveled to work for meetings and other special events. The work program allowed her to regain a relatively normal lifestyle, a lifestyle she had been without for some time. In addition she refreshed her computer skills and management expertise in a work environment with which she was quite comfortable. With time she was able to re-enter the labour market full time. Throughout the process she relied on a psychologist to assist in developing strategies to manage her thoughts and feelings and prepare herself to re-enter the workforce.

Motivation

In the above case study, the employee demonstrated marked motivation despite having been off work for two years. Clearly, the employer's delay in working with this individual could have adversely affected the employee's desire to participate in the various initiatives.

In many instances an employee's motivation is tied directly to how they perceive a given situation. In the above case study, the employee was left to fend for herself for two years. Employee/employer contact was limited. The employee felt isolated and without support. This is a very common scenario. Indeed, the more time that the employee has to think about the treatment received, the more opportunity there is to develop resentment that can lead to isolation and limited co-operation. This type of scenario can develop via a multitude of situations including an employee/supervisor conflict, low employee morale or limited communication between management and labour. Limiting the amount of discontent among your employees can lead to better motivation.

Vocational Goals

For most disabled employees, dealing with a temporary or permanent disability is difficult at the best of times. Generally speaking, they have no experience in or knowledge of coping or managing the issues that they must deal with on a day-to-day basis. Realizing they may never perform the activities they did prior to their disability can be daunting. This, coupled with the knowledge that they will need to identify alternate work can be a lot to handle.

Taking these factors into account is crucial to successfully proceeding throughout the vocational rehabilitation process. Without exception the more buy-in your employee has in terms of identifying new occupations, the more success the employee will have in returning to work in a suitable job they feel good about.

To this end it is important to gain as much insight into the worker's interests as possible. Generally speaking, when identifying suitable employment opportunities, there are two groups of employees: goal-directed and undirected.

Goal Directed

Goal-directed employees have definite ideas about what other job opportunities they can pursue. Within this group are those employees who have a realistic view of what jobs are available and suitable, taking into account their skills and abilities. They understand that the job opportunities they are considering must reasonably reflect the realities of their pre-disability occupation. In other words, an employee earning $12 an hour would not be retrained to secure work paying $20 an hour. Conversely, an employee who has worked all his life in a single location should not be expected to travel out of town as part of his job unless the employee is willing to do this. Regular communication with the employee will improve your ability to better understand what the employee is motivated to do.

Within the goal-directed group are also disabled employees who believe their disability should entitle them to financial assistance to significantly upgrade their skills. Employees in this group usually require only an explanation of the goal of the vocational rehabilitation process, which is to minimize the disability's current or future impact on the employee's ability to participate or earn a standard of living comparable to that which he or she had before the disability.

Undirected

Most disabled employees have no vocational goals. They are undirected. In many cases they have no ideas or interests that can be translated into potential job options. In many cases, this is due to the fact that they remain overwhelmed by the fact that they are unable to return to their pre-disability job. A career change is an issue most people rarely, if ever, consider.

When an employee has little or no idea about what his or her interests are, either vocationally or otherwise, it is prudent to seek out the services of a vocational rehabilitation specialist. The specialist will gain the necessary information through interviewing and testing. The specialist can then begin to identify suitable employment options. Refer to Chapter 5 for more information about vocational rehabilitation service providers.

TOOLS

Once it is determined that an employee is unable to return to work with the pre-disability employer because of a disability, vocational rehabilitation services are required.

Listed below are a few of the tools most commonly used by a vocational rehabilitation specialist or case manager to assess, match and recommend suitable employment options. This is not a comprehensive list as a number of tools are beyond the scope of this book.

Transferable Skills Analysis

The transferable skills analysis is a detailed description of the employee's previous work history, both paid and unpaid, and interests and other activities that could potentially lead to a suitable job opportunity. Key to assessing the employee's interests and abilities is an open discussion about the employee's daily activities. Clearly, the discussion should focus on the activities that the employee does most. For most, paid employment is their primary source of skill development. By thoroughly evaluating each skill as they pertain to the employee's experiences, you will be successful in identifying the employee's skills and abilities. This in turn can be used to match the employee to an appropriate job.

> **TIP:** *Ask your employee for an updated résumé to assist in determining where he or she has worked in the past and what skills and abilities he or she has learned since being hired.*

When considering what skills can be transferred from one occupation to another, be as thorough as possible. For example, a machine operator may have problem-solving skills, hand-eye co-ordination, fine finger manipulation skills and an ability to follow directions or work orders. All of these skills are transferable.

For some employees virtually all of the work history has been focused on one occupation. In this situation the probability of identifying a suitable job will be more difficult. It is particularly important in this case to draw upon the employee's unpaid work skills developed via volunteer work, hobbies or interests. There are a number of volunteer activities that should be investigated: church activities, cultural or community association activities or coaching activities. In each of these cases the employee will have skills above and beyond the skills gained through paid work experience. Transferable skills are unique to the individual. The more skills analyses you completed during the assessment phase, the more success in matching the employee's skills, abilities and interests to a job.

A sample transferable skills analysis form is included at Form 7 in the Appendix.

Vocational Assessment

From the transferable skills analysis it should become apparent whether the employee has the necessary skills to re-enter the labour market directly, taking into account their skills, previous earnings and physical abilities. If it is determined that it is unlikely that the employee will be successful in restoring his or her pre-disability wage without upgrading, more testing may be required.

CASE STUDY

A 45-year-old assembly line worker can no longer perform that type of work due to a progressively degenerating disc problem. She previously earned $15 an hour. Her employer considered placing her in another job, however, they were unable to accommodate her back limitations. A transferable skills analysis is completed and it is determined that while she has a number of transferable skills, all of the jobs for which she is qualified from a skill perspective are physically unsuitable. The case manager determined that the worker would need to develop new skills to be successful in securing a job that takes advantage of her physical abilities and skills while maximizing her earnings potential. The case manager arranges for a vocational evaluation to determine what the employee's learning abilities are both in terms of learning on the job and participating in a formal training program.

Evaluation will consider the employee's motivation levels, interests, language skills, previous formal training (*i.e.*, high school and post-secondary education), the ability to follow instructions, vocational interests, thinking skills and physical abilities. The results of the psychometric testing along with previous work experience will be used to determine what job options are available to the employee, taking into account learning skills.

If the employee has the ability to successfully complete a formal training program, the potential loss of earnings can be minimized. The disability would then have less financial impact on the ability to resume work. If the worker is not a suitable candidate for formal training, on-the-job training or job options that require non-academic (hands on) skill development may be possible.

When an employee is unable to restore their pre-disability earnings, a third party insurance provider is usually involved, such as a workers' compensation board or a long-term disability insurance provider, depending on the terms of the policy. The transferable skills analysis and the vocational assessment will be used by the insurance carrier to determine what, if any, loss of earnings may result due to the employee's physical disability.

Psycho-Vocational Assessment

When an employee is having difficulty dealing with the psychological and/or emotional aspect of a disability, the employee may benefit from a psycho-vocational assessment. In addition to obtaining information provided in the vocational evaluation, psychological issues are also considered. A psycho-vocational assessment may be appropriate if the employee is having difficulty managing pain or believes he or she will be unable to re-enter the labour market. This assessment includes a meeting with a psychologist. The meeting is used to gain a better understanding of the employee's perceptions pertaining to the labour market re-entry process. The psychologist will also review with the employee the aptitude, interests and intelligence tests completed during the vocational assessment.

Work Sample Assessment

The work sample assessment is used to gain further insight into an employee's aptitudes and interests. It is a less commonly used tool, however, quite effective in helping the case manager and the disabled employee gain a better perspective of the duties and skills required to perform a given job.

A work sample is completed at a supervised test centre, not in a conventional work setting. The assessment provides both the case manager and the disabled employee with further insight as to whether an occupation is viable. Work samples are particularly effective when the employee has expressed interest in a job but has not actually performed the activities typically associated with the job. The employee performs simulated work over a two or three-hour period. Most private vocational assessment centres can offer a number of work samples pertaining to a wide range of occupations including electronic repair, reception work, sheet metal, managerial and clerical work. In the case of a receptionist, work activities would include filing, typing, message taking, answering a multi-line telephone and following verbal and written instructions.

The work sample tool is typically done in conjunction with other assessment tools.

Situational Assessment

Situational assessments, in contrast to a work sample, allow the employee to perform real work in a real work environment. Just like a work sample, a situational assessment is performed in a controlled environment, meaning an evaluator pays close attention to what the person participating in the assessment is doing in terms of productivity, attendance, punctuality and work behaviours. Unlike the work sample, which is done over a few hours, the situational assessment usually is done over several days or weeks to gain an accurate view of the employee's ability to perform a given job full time.

Situational assessments are used to confirm if an employee is employable. If you suspect your disabled employee is unable to work full time, a situational assessment is an excellent means of objectively determining what the employee is capable of without placing him or her in an unsafe or overwhelming situation.

PERMANENTLY DISABLED EMPLOYEE'S PSYCHOLOGICAL NEEDS

When a permanently disabled employee is unable to return to his or her regular job or a comparable job, a number of psychological variables need to be considered. Some of these variables will require professional intervention, however, employers can also play a significant role in helping to address the issues that are preventing the employee from working.

While many employers do not perceive themselves as caregivers, most if not all of the health and safety training orientation an employee receives is a form of caregiving. Caregiving is due diligence. It prevents employees from causing undue harm to themselves or others. Just as a parent practises due diligence in ensuring their children avoid unhealthy or dangerous situations, so too does the employer. As a provider of due diligence, employers must consider all aspects of their employees' needs including physical, emotional and psychological health.

In the case of a permanently disabled employee, care and support are perhaps the primary considerations. If a disabled employee has reason to believe he or she will not be returning to the pre-disability occupation, the employer should demonstrate by actions and words that all reasonable steps are being taken to identify alternate work in the company.

It is not enough to *say* to the employee that no appropriate work is available, the employer must take steps to confirm this. Many employers believe that it is not their responsibility to evaluate possible alternate jobs. It should not be a question of whether the company has the expertise, time or desire to assess suitable employment options, rather it should be an automatic response to ensuring your disabled employee is receiving the care and support required from the various stakeholders. By applying best practices regardless of what issues or obstacles arise, your employees will be happier and more productive. Superior communication, labour management relations, productivity and morale will follow.

Listed below are some questions that employers need to consider when attempting to return a permanently disabled employee to work:

- What measures are in place to ensure all of the employee's physical, emotional and psychological needs are addressed?
- What, if any, financial or non-financial assistance is available through your workers' compensation or long-term disability insurance company?
- What, if any, service providers are available to assist in assessing the employee's skills and training abilities?
- Is the employee motivated to return to work and perform a different job with the same company?

SUMMARY

- Vocational rehabilitation is the process of matching an employee's physical abilities, skills, knowledge, aptitudes, interests, training and experience to an occupation.
- When determining if and when vocational rehabilitation services are necessary, consider the medical, employability, psycho-social and financial issues.
- Assessing your employee, matching employee characteristics to suitable occupations, organizing job preparation and job placement are key components to rehabilitating your employee.
- When using external service providers, clearly determine what your needs are, select a service provider that will satisfy your needs, and clearly document the questions you want answered by the provider.

- When assessing employability, consider the employee's physical abilities, productivity, punctuality and attendance, learning abilities, and psycho-social, motivational and vocational goals.
- The transferable skills analysis identifies the employee's skills, abilities and experiences by gaining a detailed understanding of the employee's disability and work history, personal information such as date of birth, country of origin, languages spoken, and educational qualifications (such as licences and designations).
- Transferable skills analysis, vocational assessment, psycho-vocational assessment, work sample assessment and situational assessment are the most commonly used vocational rehabilitation tools.
- Identifying the psychological issues that affect your employee's ability to return to work and planning an action plan are just as important as identifying occupational goals.

REVIEW QUESTIONS

1. List three variables that need to be considered in determining whether a vocational evaluation is warranted.
2. Name four elements required to quantify employability.
3. What are the essential elements of a transferable skills analysis?

CHAPTER 4

Disability Management
Policy and Procedures

LEARNING OBJECTIVES

By the end of this chapter, you should have an understanding of:

- letters of intent
- goal and objective statements
- disability management policy and procedure statements
- stakeholder roles and responsibilities
- how to write a dispute resolution procedure
- how to incorporate workers' compensation, short-term and long-term disability considerations into your policy and procedures

INTRODUCTION

Clearly, employers that support the notion that their employees are their most valuable asset have a far better chance of returning disabled employees to work than those that do not.

The National Institute for Disability Management and Research's ("NIDMAR") guide, *Disability Management in the Workplace: A Guide to Establishing a Joint Workplace Program,*[1] outlines a number of sample documents used by organizations that have successfully established a disability management program. The following is an excerpt from that guide.

---

[1] National Institute for Disability Management and Research, *Disability Management in the Workplace: A Guide to Establishing a Joint Workplace Program*, S. Riessner, ed. (Fort Alberni, B.C., 1995).

Letter of Intent
     BETWEEN **MacMillan Bloedel Limited**
                   Somass Division
     AND   **International Woodworkers of America - Canada**
                   Local 1-85
     PURPOSE **Disability Management**

Both parties recognize the need to more effectively deal with employees who may be affected by a disability. As such, they agree to develop and implement an effective Joint Union/Management Disability program which will re-integrate people back to a productive capacity.

The attached proposal reflects the framework expected but ultimately, the end product will be jointly agreed to.

If there are any difficulties which may be encountered, both parties will endeavor to resolve them as expediently as possible.

Signed on behalf of: Signed on behalf of:

_____   _____

IWA - CANADA Local 1-85   MacMILLAN BLOEDEL LIMITED
                               SOMASS DIVISION[2]

It is one thing to have a disability management program, it is quite another to have a program that ensures the time you have invested in designing the program is time well spent. Your goal and objective statement is key to ensuring that your disability management program is doing what you want it to do. These statements will assist you in evaluating your program on a quarterly and annual basis.

Your objectives should be "SMART":

S pecific
M easurable
A ttainable
R ealistic
T imed

The following goal statements can be applied company wide or by department or plant. Efforts should be made to evaluate the appropriateness of each goal and objective according to each plant or department. It should not be assumed that the strengths and weaknesses of each plant or

---

[2] *Ibid.*, at p. 70. Reproduced with permission.

department are the same. Every department and plant has its own unique needs based on demographics and other considerations.

Sample goal statements:
- To reduce lost-time claim costs (workers' compensation, short and long-term disability) from (current total hard and soft costs) to (estimated cost of having to implement a disability management program)
- To reduce the duration of claims from (current average length of claim) to (projected length of claim after implementing the disability management program)
- To reduce the frequency of (claim type) from (number of instances per month, quarter or year) to (estimated number of instances per month, quarter or year after implementing the disability management program)

Sample objective statements:
- To contact all absent disabled employees within 24 hours of lost time to obtain physical abilities information, develop a return-to-work plan and determine benefit entitlement
- To obtain physician endorsement of the return-to-work plan within seven days of completing the return-to-work plan
- To have physical abilities information, physical demands analysis and initial assessment report on file within five days of lost-time date.

WRITING A POLICY

Characteristics of a good policy and procedure statement:

- policy objective (what do you hope to accomplish)
- when it takes effect (including the effective date and review date)
- where it applies (is it company wide or plant specific?)
- to whom it applies (does the policy apply to all bargaining units or all employees or full-time employees with three months of service?)
- why you need the policy (what is the rationale for changing or adding this policy to your existing policy?)

Consistent with the notion that employees are your most valuable asset, is that all disabled employees — whether they become disabled at or away from work — require early and proactive management to minimize both the hard and soft costs associated with employee absenteeism. The longer an employee is off work, the higher the costs.

While most organizations are constantly analyzing how they can reduce or eliminate machinery breakdown, the same cannot always be said for the employees operating those machines. It is through your policy and procedures that physical, emotional and psychological issues are addressed. Policy and procedures are the medium for achieving this.

Proactively returning *all* disabled employees to work regardless of when or where they became disabled is not as onerous as you may think. Listed in Table 4-1 are some of the key policy questions that will assist you in ensuring your disability management policy is effective, fair and consistent. By honestly answering each of these questions, you will gain some insight as to whether your policy and procedures reflect many of the best practices being used by other organizations.

Table 4-1

	Yes	No
1. Are disability management policies and procedures consistent with our corporate vision and values (*i.e.*, the promotion of self worth, maximizing the skills and abilities of our employees)?		
2. We have a process for ensuring that ongoing communication with each stakeholder occurs from the beginning of the claim until claim resolution.		
3. We have appropriate resources available to accurately assess our employees' physical, emotional and psychological needs.		
4. We offer graduated return to work, workstation modifications and other appropriate return-to-work assistance to all disabled employees regardless of when or where the disability occurred.		
5. We work co-operatively with all stakeholders to proactively return all our employees to work in a timely fashion.		
6. We monitor stakeholder compliance to our policy and procedures.		
7. We provide standardized information sheets to all our employees explaining our values, policies and stakeholder responsibilities.		

	Yes	No
8. We make it easy for all disabled employees to maintain contact with our case manager, supervisor and/or other service providers to facilitate an early and safe return to work (*i.e.*, information sheets with telephone numbers, an outline of employee responsibilities as they pertain to return-to-work initiatives).		
9. Our disability management values, principles, policy and procedures are included in collective bargaining agreements and other labour management agreements.		
10. The nature of the disability and claim type (*i.e.*, occupational or non-occupational) is not a factor in determining eligibility for the disability management program.		
11. We use multiple mediums to educate and train internal and external stakeholders about our disability management program.		
12. We handle return-to-work disputes quickly and efficiently.		
13. All stakeholders have a clear understanding of their responsibilities.		
14. Our policy and procedures were developed taking into account all the key stakeholders.		

STAKEHOLDERS

Key to establishing effective disability management procedures is stakeholder identification. The more you understand the processes and the stakeholders involved, the more success you will have.

Generally speaking, there are three primary stakeholders: the disabled employee, the employer (usually a manager) and the attending health care provider. These stakeholders have been identified as primary, to reflect the fact that they all must be involved in the return-to-work process.

Secondary stakeholders work in co-operation with the primary stakeholders to efficiently return the disabled employee to work. This group of stakeholders may include a union representative, benefits adjudicator or adjuster, and specialty service provider such as a physiotherapist.

Depending on the corporation, the case manager may be appointed internally or externally. The responsibilities of the case manager can be performed by a human resources or health and safety professional. By combining the roles of employer representative and case manager you gain in having a case manager who understands many of the issues only an employee can appreciate. In turn, the manager can use this knowledge to effectively manage the claim. Conversely, by combining these positions you lose the expertise an external provider can provide. Depending on the complexity of the claim, that expertise can significantly affect the success of your return-to-work efforts. In addition, an external case manager can give the disabled employee some peace of mind knowing that his interests and perspective will be considered in an objective fashion. If you opt for an internal case manager, consider having the case manager participate in some training to help them fully address the difficult task of managing a disability claim. Training programs are available through a number of community colleges and private organizations such as NIDMAR.[3]

Primary Stakeholder Responsibilities

Disabled Employee

In most cases the disabled employee is responsible for the following:

- reporting incidences of lost time to their designated supervisor or manager
- obtaining, in a timely fashion, employee functional abilities information
- maintaining ongoing communication with the designated case manager and other stakeholders
- reporting any material change in physical or emotional or psychological condition that may affect the return-to-work plan
- assisting in the identification of suitable employment opportunities
- assisting in the design and development of a return-to-work plan
- actively participating in any rehabilitation activities that will assist in facilitating a return to work

Employer Representative

Depending on the design of your disability management program, you may have more than one employer representative. In any case, the employer is responsible for organizing the following in co-operation with the other stakeholders.

---

[3]   NIDMAR website is: www.nidmar.ca.

Program responsibilities:
- forming a steering committee
- establishing program parameters (goals, objectives, principles and practices)
- gaining buy-in from the other stakeholders
- explaining stakeholder roles and responsibilities
- program promotion and education
- conforming to legislation
- program evaluation

Case management:
- communicating with the disabled employee and other stakeholders throughout the period of lost time
- assessing the disabled employee's needs and matching his or her abilities to a job
- gathering data from internal and external stakeholders
- interpreting medical and non-medical information
- monitoring return-to-work plans and rehabilitation activities
- distinguishing between objective and subjective information
- identifying and addressing return-to-work obstacles
- developing a return-to-work plan
- setting goals and priorities
- identifying and referring disabled employees to external service providers
- evaluating program successes and failures
- negotiating and organizing alternative dispute resolution
- maintaining file documentation

Family Physician

The family physician's role in returning a disabled employee to work is ensuring that the employee receives timely and appropriate medical attention. Generally speaking, physicians are trained to diagnose medical conditions and provide the necessary support either through referral or primary care to ensure the employee is capable of resuming all or most of his or her daily pre-disability activities.

A family physician devotes much of his or her time to providing medical care. The physician does not venture into other disciplines such as vocational rehabilitation or return-to-work case management activities.

The physician understands the limits of his or her expertise and avoids delving into outside issues.

Physician responsibilities in most instances should be limited to:

- quantifying physical abilities
- organizing medical treatment or specialist appointments/consultations
- monitoring and evaluating treatment plans to ensure employees are progressing toward return-to-work objectives

Secondary Stakeholder Responsibilities

Union Representative

The union representative is generally responsible for the following:

- ensuring the disability management program conforms to legislative obligations and collective bargaining agreements
- representing or providing guidance and insight into issues of concern to the disabled employee
- assisting and participating in the design and evaluation of the disability management program

Benefits Adjudicator

The benefits or claims adjudicator's responsibilities include determining benefit entitlement and facilitating a resolution. This is usually achieved by ongoing contact with the disabled employee and other stakeholders. When determining claim entitlement they consider the following:

- Does the claim satisfy all the legislative or policy conditions required to be compensable?
- Assuming the claim is compensable, is it reasonable to conclude the employee requires time off work to obtain or participate in rehabilitative activities designed to return the employee to work?
- What activities are required to return the employee to his or her pre-disability lifestyle? What is the duration of the activities?
- Is there reason to believe that the employee will not be capable of returning to their pre-disability lifestyle? If yes, what activities are required to ensure the employee regains most of his or her pre-disability activities?

Specialty Service Providers

Assessment services

Assessment services provide specific assessments and recommendations that extend beyond the skills and abilities of the primary stakeholders. Assessors provide consultative information that can be used as a means of providing specific information and education to one or more of the key stakeholders (*e.g.*, an independent medical evaluation or ergonomic assessment).

Dispute resolution services

Dispute, regardless of how or why it was initiated, is a necessary part of an effective disability management program. Indeed, almost without exception, stakeholder disputes will arise. Developing procedures that will assist in expeditiously addressing disputes will benefit everyone. As previously discussed, communication, co-operation and commitment to the process are crucial.

The following questions will assist you in working through a dispute:

1. Do you have an accurate understanding of the issue(s) in dispute taking into consideration the opinions of all stakeholders?
2. Do all the participants have an understanding of the dispute process? For example:
    - What are the timelines (start and end dates)?
    - How will a mediator be selected?
    - Are all stakeholders involved in establishing mediator responsibilities and powers?
    - How and when will appeals be considered?
    - How many levels of appeal will be provided? (*e.g.*, line supervisor, department manager, senior management)
    - Is an external service provider capable of providing objective solutions that all stakeholders will respect and abide by?
    - What control measures are in place to ensure all disputes are handled consistently and efficiently and without fear of reprisal? (*e.g.*, all referred disputes will be addressed within five days of referral beginning with the immediate supervisor)
    - What evaluation protocols have been built into the dispute resolution process to streamline or to make it more efficient?

- What complement of service providers will be required to address the various dispute issues? (*e.g.*, medical, case management, psychological, collective bargaining, legislative, policy interpretation)
3. What other formal dispute mechanisms may affect your internal process?

PROGRAM ELIGIBILITY AND EXIT POLICY/PROCEDURE

Managing a disability management program can be onerous and time-consuming. As a result, the program should not be used without some consideration. The following questions will help you consider when an employee should be referred to your disability management program.

> **TIP**: *Remember, these eligibility considerations are not driven by legislative obligations such as worker compensation legislation, rather they reflect the best practice of doing everything reasonably possible to promote the emotional, physical and psychological health of your most valuable assets, your employees. By demonstrating this level of commitment to your employees you increase productivity and morale and reduce turnover and claim frequency and duration.*

Eligibility criteria considerations:
- Is the employee unable to work full or part time due to physical, emotional or psychological disability?
- Is the employee unable to maintain acceptable productivity levels due to illness, emotional, psychological or physical disability? (*E.g.*, The employee may attend work daily but is unable to work efficiently during the course of the day.)
- Does a new employee require a workstation modification to perform his or her job?
- Is a workstation adversely affecting your employees' abilities to achieve their full productivity potential? (*E.g.*, is the workstation ergonomically inefficient resulting in repetitive body motion and muscle fatigue?)
- Has the employee previously abused the program?
- Is the employee eligible or receiving other disability management services greater or equal to the company program?

Exit considerations:

- Is it reasonable to conclude that the employee will retire on or before he or she has been rehabilitated?
- Is it likely the employee will be incapable of performing his or her pre-disability job, a comparable job or a suitable job?
- The employee requires comprehensive health care services that will deem him or her unemployable for an extended period of time (*i.e.*, a month or longer).
- The employee is not co-operating with the previously agreed-upon plan.
- Has the employee experienced a significant life disruption (*i.e.*, a death) while participating in the disability management program and become eligible for other benefits?
- The employee returns to work with the pre-disability employer or another employer.

WORKERS' COMPENSATION, SHORT AND LONG-TERM DISABILITY

As mentioned above, customizing your disability management program to meet your organizational needs — as opposed to legislative obligations — can result in an increase in employee morale and productivity and reduce lost-time claims and turnover. Many employers believe that by addressing their legal obligations, they are doing everything reasonably possible to control costs associated with employee absences due to disability. Ironically, it is precisely the opposite that is true. Indeed, by addressing your organizational needs first, your legislative obligations will take care of themselves. Clearly, the more emphasis you place on maintaining a happy, healthy workforce, the easier it will be to exceed government legislation.

Listed below are some of the obligations to which employers are required to adhere. As you will see, the principles reflected in these statements should be occurring not because employers are obligated to do so but because they make good business sense to do so.

Ontario workers' compensation and human rights legislation require:

- communication with disabled employees throughout the period of disability
- matching and offering employment that is consistent with the employee's physical, emotional and psychological needs

91

- job accommodation
- not to discriminate based on disability

Short-Term Disability

Generally speaking, management of short-term disability resides with the employer. For that reason it is not uncommon for employers to have little or no structure, policy or procedure associated with this benefit. This can result in a relatively straightforward claim becoming a prolonged and complicated disability claim.

Below are some key questions that will assist you in determining what you are doing well as they pertain to management of your STD claims and what aspects of your program require further consideration.

- Is the absence related to disability or illness? (*E.g.*, is it reasonable to think the claim will extend for several weeks or months?)
- What impact is your STD program design having on the success of your disability management program?

If your STD program allows employees to accumulate sick days and carry them forward, what provisions are in place to ensure employees are using sick days legitimately? In some cases employees may have hundreds of sick days banked. What checks and balances are in place to ensure your employees are using banked sick days to rehabilitate rather than to take time off?

While an employee may see no harm in extending a period of absence from work for weeks or months beyond what would have been considered reasonable, a day lost beyond what is considered reasonable results in significant employer expense. By establishing reasonable recovery timelines, you will improve your program efficiency thereby reducing costs and you will be perceived by management and labour as being consistently fair.

Long-Term Disability

When a claim surpasses the six-month mark, it is typically regarded as a long-term disability. These claims are usually the most complex as the longevity of the claim can result in related issues such as chronic pain or depression. These issues require a multi-disciplinary approach, which adds to the complexity of the claim. It is not uncommon for an employee off work for this period of time to perceive himself as unemployable.

Clearly, it is better to avoid having claims that extend beyond the six-month mark. To do this, everything reasonably possible must be done early on in the claim. Very few claims should result in a six-month or more absence. Use the list below to gain a better appreciation for initiatives that should be taken to facilitate a return to work.

1. *Is your LTD provider proactively managing the claim to facilitate a return to work?*
Chances are your LTD provider is monitoring the claim with the intention of containing their costs. Little or no provisions are in place to evaluate the appropriateness of the services the disabled employee is receiving. For example, a physiotherapist may have the necessary resources to manage most if not all muscle and bone disabilities, however, it is exceptional to have a clinic understand the complexities of how an employee's physical needs can impact their psychological needs. They simply do not have the complement of staff to manage complex cases effectively. Those employees who suffer from multiple impairments do not respond to standardized treatment programs; customization is necessary to restore function and to facilitate a return to work.

2. *What, if any, assistance has your LTD provider given you to ensure everything that can be done is being done to return your employee to work?*
Insurance carriers enjoy significant knowledge about virtually every aspect of disability management. Indeed, this knowledge is extremely valuable to employers interested in maximizing their efforts in returning disabled employees to work. Any value-added services that your provider offers can also enhance your ability to minimize the number of long-term claims you experience over a year. This will positively impact your experience rating (see Glossary).

3. *What, if any, performance statistics are available from your LTD provider that will assist you in better understanding your claims?*
By understanding why your employees are collecting LTD benefits, you will be in a better situation to understand what, if anything, can be done within the plant or workplace to better control or eliminate the variables that result in claims. There are many variables that can contribute to LTD claims. In the case of stress-related disability,

downsizing, job layoffs, amalgamation and poor management can all lead to increased incidence of LTD claims.

Other variables that should be considered when evaluating your provider's ability to manage claims is the duration of each claim, gender issues (women tend to be off work more than men), common return-to-work barriers such as communication between stakeholders, and the effectiveness of services received by the disabled employee.

4.   *What, if any, preferred provider network is available to assist you in managing all your claims?*

In most instances, LTD carriers have a plethora of service providers in all regions to address the needs of the disabled employee. In gaining access to this network of services you will likely gain not only a number of community service providers but also providers who have demonstrated an ability to deliver their services at a pre-defined level.

SUMMARY

- The letter of intent should be used to gain initial buy-in from all stakeholders including the union and upper management.
- Goals and objectives should be SMART and need-specific. The more you understand the needs according to the plant or department, the more successful your program will be.
- Policy and procedures should be written only after it is clear what the need is.
- Involve all stakeholders in defining roles and responsibilities. The more involved they are the more committed they will be to making a positive contribution to the program.
- Disputes will occur. A clear dispute policy will reduce inefficiency and allow you to resolve disputes quickly and equitably.
- Legislative obligations are minimum standards, they should not be used to establish best practices or policy. By raising the standards that your organization uses to conduct its day-to-day affairs, you will reduce costs and begin to establish the kind of work environment leading organizations strive for.

REVIEW QUESTIONS

1. Why is buy-in important to establishing and running a good disability management program?
2. Name five stakeholders and explain their roles and responsibilities.
3. Name three external service providers and outline what services they can provide.

CHAPTER 5

Community Service Providers

LEARNING OBJECTIVES

By the end of this chapter, you should have an understanding of:

- types of service providers
- when to use a service provider
- how to select a service provider who meets your needs
- issues to consider when negotiating a preferred service provider arrangement
- how to write a service provider contract
- how to evaluate your service provider's performance

INTRODUCTION

Regardless of how big or small your company is, sooner or later you will require the services of an external service provider. Fundamental to this is the recognition that most organizations simply do not have the skills or expertise in human resources to address all their management needs.

This chapter focuses on the various service providers with which small and large organizations should be familiar when managing employee disability. Whether you contract out the management of your disability program or not, it is prudent to become familiar with the issues identified in this chapter. In turn you will be much more able to fully consider your needs in selecting providers and also evaluating your provider's ability to serve your needs.

TYPES OF SERVICE PROVIDERS

As we have discussed, managing employee disability requires a multi-disciplined approach regardless of the seriousness of the disability. Disability impacts not only the employee's physical abilities but also the employee's emotional and psychological well-being. For this reason it is important to ensure this fundamental principle is reflected in your disability management program. While every employee and every disability is different, by considering all of the employee's needs — whether physiotherapy, psychotherapy, counselling, education or a combination of these — from the beginning you will almost certainly avoid the unanticipated events that tend to arise during the return-to-work process. As you gain experience and expertise in identifying the red flags that appear, you will become more efficient at ensuring that all your employee's needs are being addressed.

CASE STUDY
Joe injured his back lifting machine parts. He had previously been off work with a similar, non-work-related back injury. Joe's supervisor was convinced that he was using his most recent injury as a means of extending his holiday time. It was widely known that Joe was not happy in his current position.
Case study facts: low paying, high turnover job, physically demanding job responsibilities and low employee morale.

This case study will be revisited below as we examine how the various service providers might handle Joe's scenario.

The following providers are listed in no particular order. Depending on the facts and complexities of the claim in question, a case manager may rely on one or more of the providers listed.

- surveillance provider
- independent evaluator
- physiotherapist
- attending physician
- external case manager
- exercise therapist
- kinesiologist

Surveillance Providers

The use of surveillance equipment (*i.e.*, audio and video), while never conclusive, can help confirm or rule out issues in dispute. Having clear objectives or questions will enhance your ability to acquire the information that you require. In the above case study, a surveillance provider could confirm or deny Joe's activities while off work. The provider could confirm whether the employee was indeed actively participating in the agreed-upon return-to-work activities.

Consider the following before retaining the services of a surveillance contractor:

- Cost of service versus the potential value the information will provide. For example, how likely is it that the surveillance information will assist in reducing or eliminating your current costs and future claim costs? Will the surveillance costs be equal to or less than your total claim costs?
- What are the possible ramifications of using such a service (*e.g.*, deterioration of employee/management relations)?
- What, if any, policy and procedures are in place to assist the supervisor or manager in knowing under what circumstances a surveillance provider should be used?
- What is the probability of obtaining the information you require by using this type of service? (Discuss this with the contractor.)
- How much surveillance time will be required to obtain the information required?

Independent Evaluators

Independent evaluations are used primarily to gain an unbiased perspective on a given set of facts. There are many types of evaluations and many types of practitioners. Table 5-1 summarizes the most common types of evaluations and associated practitioners.

Table 5-1

Evaluation or Assessment Type	Practitioner Title
Independent medical evaluation	Orthopaedic surgeon, psychologist, psychiatrist, neurologist, physiatrist
Post-offer placement evaluation	Kinesiologist, occupational therapist
Functional abilities evaluation	Physiotherapist, occupational therapist
Work site evaluation	Kinesiologist, occupational therapist
Vocational evaluation	Vocational evaluator or vocational rehabilitation specialist
Psycho-vocational evaluation	Psychologist, vocational evaluator
Transferable skills analysis	Vocational evaluator or vocational rehabilitation specialist
Situational assessment	Vocational evaluator or vocational rehabilitation specialist

Physiotherapist

The physiotherapist is responsible for assessing, recommending and implementing a physical treatment program on behalf of the disabled employee. In addition, the physiotherapist may be involved in co-ordinating the employee's treatment program (*e.g.*, a referral to a behavioural therapist or massage therapist).

Attending Physician

If the employee requires time off work, the attending physician is usually the first external service provider the disabled employee will contact. The physician should not be viewed as an employee advocate, but rather as a source of important medical information that will assist in proactively returning the disabled employee to work. The attending physician can provide you with critical information that in turn can be used to effect an early and safe return to work.

There are two keys to obtaining pertinent information. First, understand the scope of the physician's expertise. If you understand the physician's abilities and knowledge base you will be much more capable of obtaining the information (*i.e.*, employee physical abilities) you require. Secondly, explain your intentions and willingness to co-operate — either in writing or verbally — you will be more likely to gain the support of the physician. Keep in mind that in many instances the attending physician has little or no knowledge about what the disabled employee is required to do. As a result, the physician rightly errs on the side of caution rather than making assumptions about how safe a return to work would be for the employee.

Some multi-disciplined external service providers have a host of staff. Often this type of facility allows the employer and external service provider to be more efficient, thus eliminating or reducing the amount of information sharing required. For example, if an organization can rely on a few multidisciplinary providers (family physician, physiotherapist, occupational therapist and other specialists) to manage the bulk of their claims, the need for repeatedly sharing job descriptions or modified work program details is reduced. The providers become much more in tune with the jobs, the employees and the machines. Conversely, if every disabled employee relied on a physician who had little or no understanding of the company and its disability management program, the process would be very inefficient. This is not to say that your disabled employee should be directed to use specific external service providers, rather he should be given the choice of using of his or her own provider or using a provider identified by the employer. If the benefits of using a preferred service provider are explained to Joe, he will most likely choose it.

By using the preferred provider:

- the employee will enjoy superior treatment due to staff that have a better understanding of job demands
- there will be less time off work
- there will be improved communication between stakeholders

External Case Manager

In our case study, Joe's employer was concerned about potential abuse of the system. A case manager can serve as an effective resource person to contact internal and external stakeholders to determine what the issues are and proactively manage the claim. A number of organizations utilize external case managers to benefit from the arm's length relationship they enjoy with disabled employees. The case manager's expertise in gathering information can be helpful in fully understanding and addressing all the issues that are affecting the employee's ability to work.

101

The external case manager generally has more opportunity and skill to properly evaluate necessary external service providers and provide timely intervention through the life of the claim, thereby minimizing claim duration.

Based on Joe's scenario the external case manager could assess his return-to-work needs, identify, retain and manage the necessary service providers and facilitate a return to work.

Exercise Therapist

Depending on Joe's needs, an exercise therapist could be used to educate and train him on strengthening muscle groups and maintaining a level of fitness that minimizes the potential of future strains or disability.

Kinesiologist

If it appears the nature of Joe's disability is associated with the design of the workstation, a kinesiologist can be quite helpful in pinpointing ergonomic issues. The kinesiologist will assess the workstation, taking into account the inefficient body postures and movements. The kinesiologist will provide recommendations that will minimize the frequency of awkward operator positioning thereby reducing or eliminating the probability of future injuries and disability.

WHEN TO USE A SERVICE PROVIDER

As mentioned, no organization has all the resources required to effectively handle all aspects of managing employee disability. As a result, external service providers are retained to provide the necessary skills and expertise to assess needs, recommend an action plan and implement the solution. Inherent in identifying a service provider is pinpointing the specific issues. Often organizations do not think this process through, which results in purchasing more than is needed. This can easily be avoided by preplanning. By establishing your needs, you can assess what services are required. From there you can determine what external providers are required.

Use the following steps to plan your needs. This five-step process can be used regardless of how simple or complex the project may be:

Step 1: What are your needs?
Step 2: Define your project scope (*i.e.*, budget, timelines, staff responsibilities).
Step 3: What internal resources are available to meet your needs?
Step 4: What external resources are available?
Step 5: How will the project be evaluated?

SELECTING A SERVICE PROVIDER TO MEET YOUR NEEDS

The person requesting the service provider should critically analyze the organization's needs. The more understanding the individual or organization has about the issue at hand the more likely they will be in retaining the providers needed to address the issue.

Listed below are a number of variables you should consider when selecting an external service provider. These variables are oriented towards issues that need to be considered when selecting a service provider for the purposes of proactively returning a disabled employee to work.

Determine Your Needs

By using the five W's (who, what, where, why, when) to answer this question you can be assured that all the issues that need addressing will be addressed.

A common scenario is referring a disabled employee to an assessment centre. In this case the *who* is the disabled employee and the evaluator. You want to understand as much as possible about the person being referred, such as languages spoken, pain behaviours if any, co-operation level, type of disability, length of time off work, job responsibilities and ability to travel. Equally important is knowing the evaluator. Find out what skills, professional designations, association memberships and experience the evaluator has, as well as contributions made to their industry such as publications or presentations. If possible, request that the evaluator contact you to discuss your needs. Most evaluators welcome the opportunity to discuss the case to gain a better understanding of your priorities and expectations.

The *what* refers to the services you require (*e.g.*, a functional abilities evaluation). Accurately assess the employee's needs immediately after the commencement of the disability; you will be ahead of the game in knowing what services you require and when you require them.

When is about co-ordination:

- When is the employee available to participate (*e.g.*, is the employee concurrently participating in other rehabilitation activities)?
- When is the provider able to allocate time to evaluate? Remember the onus is on the referrer to ensure that the time and date of the evaluation is convenient for the disabled employee and any others involved in the evaluation. If an interpreter is required or a family member is involved, it is important to ensure they are all briefed on the details.

> **TIP:** *Attempt to arrange evaluation or special assessment when the employee is not participating in other rehabilitation activities. By going out of your way for the disabled employee, the employee will be motivated to go out of his or her way for you.*

Particularly important in this scenario is the *where*. If the disabled employee is required to attend a community service provider for an assessment, clearly some consideration should be given to the distance the employee will need to travel to participate in the evaluation. In some cases it is better to spend the extra money to have the service provider come to you rather than to have the employee travel long distances. The more travel the employee is required to do, the less accurate and valid the evaluation will be. Consider the employee's perspective. If you had to travel an hour or more to and from an evaluation centre that you had never been to before while enduring pain, how prepared would you be to participate in a battery of physical activities? By minimizing the travel time, you will get an accurate evaluation and the employee will be grateful you took the time to consider his or her needs.

Finally, by assessing *why* you are referring the employee for the evaluation, you will gain a better understanding of what you expect from the assessment. For example, if the employee's job requires significant physical activity — activity that cannot be replicated in a treatment centre — a functional abilities evaluation may be in order to ensure the employee is capable of participating in a return-to-work program. By understanding the rationale for the referral, you will be well-positioned to provide the service provider with the questions you want answered. Surprisingly, many employers rely on the evaluator to provide them with the answers without giving them the insight they require to address the issues. Remember, with only a one or two-day assessment, the evaluator does not have the benefit of gaining the insight the case manager has. It is therefore important that the person making the referral gives the service provider as much detail as possible, including specific questions that can be answered based on the evaluator's skills and expertise.

PREFERRED SERVICE PROVIDER ARRANGEMENTS

Organizations big and small can benefit from a preferred service provider arrangement. Both the employer and the provider benefit. The employer receives services from a provider that has demonstrated an ability to provide one or more services. The provider is guaranteed work as a recognized preferred provider.

Much like a request for proposal, a service provider must demonstrate through a written submission that it is capable of providing the service in a way that satisfies the employer's needs. The following criterion should be used to assess external service providers:

1. How long has the provider been in business?
2. How long has the provider been providing the service you are requesting?
3. What qualifications and experience do staff have as they pertain to your given needs?
4. What provisions (human resources, equipment, accessibility) has the provider made for multiple referrals from multiple locations?
5. Is the provider responsive to your needs (*i.e.*, easy referral process, one contact to address customer service needs and take referrals, timely reports and return telephone calls, competitive rates, knowledgeable and friendly staff)?
6. Is the provider willing to customize their process to meet your needs?
7. Is the cost of the service comparable with other providers?
8. Does the provider communicate an air of professionalism to all stakeholders?
9. Are evaluation reports clear, concise and accurate?
10. Will the provider be capable of providing other services now and in the future?

11. Are the provider's premises adequate to accommodate your employees' needs (*i.e.*, wheelchair accessible, in close proximity to public transportation, convenient hours of operation, multiple language services)?
12. Is the provider willing to give customer contact names?
13. What confidentiality provisions has the contractor made to protect stakeholder privacy?
14. Does the provider have professional liability insurance? If yes, for what amount?
15. How technologically sophisticated is the provider in processing referrals and assessing and generating a report?

WRITING A SERVICE PROVIDER CONTRACT

As with any contract, it is important to include who the parties to the contract are, the responsibilities of each party, start and end dates of the contract, billing and payment provisions and dispute process and termination provisions. In addition, you may want to include performance provisions such as receiving a report within 10 days of completion of assessment or an assessment date guaranteed within five business days of referral.

Of course, obtaining the provider's signature to demonstrate agreement to the provisions is critical.

EVALUATING YOUR SERVICE PROVIDERS' PERFORMANCE

Just as you evaluate your employees' ability to perform the essential duties of their job, it is important to monitor the performance of your service providers. Your human resources — whether employees or service providers — operate in a dynamic environment. Their ability to perform can be affected by daily variables. Establishing checks and balances to address these variables will ensure appropriate steps are taken in a timely and appropriate manner.

There are five components to an effective performance review process. This applies whether you are applying it to an employee or to an external service provider. The following information focuses on evaluating the performance of an external service provider.

1. Appointment of an auditor or auditing team (the individual or group that defines performance standards for service providers and then causes the performance reviews to occur).
2. Information gathering (see the performance standards outlined in "Writing a Service Provider Contract").
3. Information analysis (comparing pre-defined performance standards to actual service provider performance, *i.e.*, did the service provider submit reports within 10 days of assessment date).
4. Providing feedback.
5. Implementing change to improve the provider's ability to achieve the pre-defined performance standards.

SUMMARY

- Using service providers can be an excellent option for employers of all sizes when they have limited or non-existent internal resources to address specific claim issues.
- Service providers offer one or more services including physiotherapy, psychotherapy, counselling and education.
- When selecting a service provider be sure to consider who the provider is, what they will be doing, when and where they will be doing it and why.
- Both large and small organizations can benefit from a preferred service provider arrangement.
- Evaluate your service providers at least once a year.

REVIEW QUESTIONS

1. Name five external service providers and summarize their responsibilities.
2. What factors are important in negotiating a service agreement?
3. Describe the five-step process used to determine whether an external service provider is required.

CHAPTER 6

Designing a Disability Management Program

LEARNING OBJECTIVES

By the end of this chapter you should have an understanding of:

- selecting a steering committee
- gaining stakeholder buy-in
- mission statements
- stakeholder responsibilities
- setting goals and objectives
- establishing guiding principles and practices
- program promotion and education
- dispute resolution
- evaluation
- confidentiality

STEERING COMMITTEE SELECTION

Key to designing and implementing a disability management program is gaining stakeholder buy-in from the beginning. One of the most effective ways of achieving this is to include the players in the program design stage. By inviting all the key stakeholders to participate in the design and development of the program, you demonstrate your commitment to addressing stakeholders' issues.

Recognizing that every stakeholder has a unique set of issues that need to be addressed will enhance the success of the program. The gains you make in working co-operatively and improving rapport during the design of your disability management program will positively impact other labour/management issues such as collective bargaining negotiations and grievance frequency.

Committee Representatives

The following steering committee questions will assist you in determining the most appropriate makeup of your committee.

- Does the committee have upper management support?
- Does your company consist of many plants or locations?
- Are you unionized?
- What kind of disability experiences does the company have (*i.e.*, muscle, stress or both)?
- Is the committee reworking an existing program or establishing a new program?
- Do all the committee members understand the value of a disability management program?
- Do labour and management respect those who have been chosen to sit on the committee?
- Will incentives be used to attract and retain committee members?
- Is the committee balanced between management and non-management staff?
- Does the committee have decision-making authority?

Committee Structure

For many organizations the committee will consist of perhaps two to four full-time staff: a disability management co-ordinator, a medical advisor (*i.e.*, employer physician, psychologist, nurse or occupational therapist), a union representative, and a previously disabled employee. If your company has multiple locations, the organization of your committee may be multi-tiered. One tier oversees the design and evaluation of the program and another tier or tiers, depending on the number of plants or office locations, oversees the management of claims at a given location. If you require a multi-tiered program, it is important to outline the scope and committee responsibilities at each tier. One of the primary mandates of the subcommittees should be to understand the needs of the stakeholders at a local level. Clearly, needs vary from location to location. Relationships between stakeholders can vary significantly from location to location: some will share a positive rapport, others will not. By addressing this or other issues early on, you will enhance the probability of success you enjoy once the program commences.

Gaining Stakeholder Buy-in

It is essential to understand that a disability management program requires a co-operative approach. Every stakeholder will have issues that, if not addressed, will result in program inefficiencies, stakeholder dissatisfaction, and ultimately program failure. Stakeholder buy-in is a process that requires building consensus among all stakeholders without exception on an ongoing basis.

There are several key points that the committee chair should consider to gain buy-in. Listed below are the essential buy-in points. Each of these points should be addressed at the local and corporate committee level.

- Recognition by all stakeholders that a disability management program makes good business sense both for the organization and its employees.
- Who should be invited to sit on the committee? (What expertise or insights into employee disability will they bring? What, if any, synergistic qualities does the individual bring to the committee? Is the individual respected by his or her peers in both management and labour?)
- What input, if any, will the committee as a whole have in selecting or overruling member nominations?
- What responsibilities and mandate will the committee have (*i.e.*, selecting a disability management co-ordinator, developing and approving policy and procedures, resolving disputes, initiating program reviews and developing best practices)?
- Will the disability management co-ordinator (chair) be an employee or an external service provider?
- How will disputes be managed?
- Will the disability management program committee be multi-tiered or centralized (*i.e.*, a multi-tiered corporate committee to manage macro issues and plant or regional committees to manage day-to-day matters)?
- Is there a training budget for members?
- Will there be mandatory training?

- What impact will the collective bargaining agreement have on the formulation of a disability management program committee and the program policy and procedures?
- Will committee members be eligible for re-election after serving their term?
- How long will committee terms be?
- Will labour/management relations in general positively or negatively impact the program?
- Will committee members be free to participate in the planning and development of the program without undue pressure from their supervisors to schedule meetings around work shifts?

MISSION STATEMENT

Understanding the needs of your disability management program through a thorough assessment of what your organization is currently doing well and what can be enhanced, will provide you with the information you need to confidently develop a mission statement.

The following list will assist you with assessing your disability management program needs.

1. Do employees and management understand the value (*i.e.*, economics, social benefits) of establishing a disability management program?
2. What mechanisms are in place to educate employees and other stakeholders about the program (*e.g.*, program principles, objectives, legislative responsibilities, eligibility criteria, exit criteria)?
3. Is it reasonable to conclude that management and labour will be capable of working co-operatively in addressing your disability management needs? If no, why not?
4. How will the introduction of a disability management program be received or interpreted by employees? (Take into account any recent mergers, acquisitions, restructuring activities.)
5. What types of disabilities are prevalent in your organization currently? Can anything can be done to address their needs? If yes, what?
6. What factors are contributing to the frequency or duration of employee lost time due to disability?

7. What can be done to minimize or eliminate these factors (*i.e.*, are disabled employees being appropriately assessed; are communication policies being adhered to by employees, supervisors and management; are external service providers providing timely information and or treatment; are your case managers able to proactively manage all lost-time claims)?

8. Are employees returning to their pre-disability job, a comparable job or a suitable job?

9. What, if any, collective bargaining provisions need to be considered when developing a disability management program?

10. Do your external service providers meet your disability management needs? Are there service gaps that impede the early and safe return to work of your disabled employees (*e.g.*, insurance carriers taking a hands-off approach until elimination period ends)?

11. What, if any, information technology systems are in place to assist in the analysis and evaluation of your lost-time claims (*i.e.*, what statistics are reviewed on a monthly basis; are case notes computerized; how is information shared among stakeholders; is information about occupational claims and non-occupational claims equally available)?

12. How does your organization's lost-time average compare with similar organizations?

13. What is your total current count of employees off work due to disability? (Include workers' compensation, short-term, long-term and motor vehicle accident claims.)

14. What are your estimated hard and soft costs due to employee disability?

15. What is your success rate both in terms of reducing lost-time claim frequency and claim duration (*i.e.*, what percentage of employees returned to full-time work after 30, 60 or 90 days)?

16. What activities have improved or inhibited your ability to help your employee have an early and safe return to work (*i.e.*, ongoing two-way communication, limited case management expertise)?

17. Do other benefit programs (*i.e.*, employee assistance program) work in co-operation with the disability management program to return disabled employees to work?

18. What job accommodations, modified work and job placement provisions are currently in place to help your disabled employees return to work? If none, why not?

In answering the above questions you will gain a better understanding of what your mission statement should be. Listed below is a sample mission statement. This statement was obtained from the National Institute of Disability Management and Research.[1]

Divisional Policy Statement for Disability Management

BETWEEN	**MacMillan Bloedel Limited**
	Somass Division
AND	**IWA - CANADA Local 1-85**

Somass Division, within the context of our vision and philosophy, recognizes that employees have:

- A "right" to a sense of belonging, identity and recognition.
- An ability to attain their untapped potential.
- A leadership role demonstrated by the application of knowledge, skill and energy.

Disability management is an effective extension of our values.

We believe that a workplace-based joint union/management approach which will enable us to re-integrate all our employees who become disabled* is the most effective strategy towards reducing the economic cost of disability and maintaining the employability of our members.

We believe that effective reintegration of disabled Somass employees minimizes the loss of expertise, resources and productive potential to the employer and is the best strategy for maintaining the employee's potential and self-worth.

The program's goal is to provide meaningful employment.

We believe that this program can be implemented and be compatible with current statutory and collective agreements (i.e., Human Rights Code and seniority application).

Current incumbency lists and seniority rights within departments as they now exist will remain.

All employees who become disabled, regardless of cause, will be eligible to participate.

*Type of disability and degree to which it affects the occupational capacity of the worker will be determined through medical assessment and work capacity evaluation.

---

[1] National Institute of Disability Management and Research, *Disability Management in the Workplace: A Guide to Establishing a Joint Workplace Program*, S. Riessner, ed. (Fort Alberni, B.C., 1995), at p. 69. Reproduced with permission.

STEERING COMMITTEE AND STAKEHOLDER RESPONSIBILITIES

Central to all good disability management programs is a good steering committee. The committee consists of those stakeholders who influence the development and management of the program. Key to ensuring all aspects of the program are considered is the selection of steering committee members. By having all stakeholders represented from the beginning, many of the issues and obstacles that impact on an employee's ability to return to work can be avoided.

The following paragraphs summarize the major responsibilities of the stakeholders typically associated with a disability management program. The descriptions are generic and therefore should be edited or enhanced based on your own needs. The more specific the responsibilities are, the greater the chance of stakeholder compliance. Also, detailed responsibilities are less subject to misinterpretation.

Disabled employee responsibilities:
- maintain contact and co-operate with the employer and other stakeholders immediately after the onset of disability and throughout the period of disability or as required to effect an early and safe return to work
- co-operate in the identification and suitability of identified job options and to be a full participant in the implementation of the return-to-work program
- participate in the design and development of a return-to-work plan
- provide functional abilities information to the employer as soon as reasonably possible for the purposes of assisting the employer in matching the employee's abilities to a suitable job

Employer (*i.e.*, disability management co-ordinator) responsibilities:
- propose and negotiate policy and procedures, goals and objectives that will guide the implementation and administration of the disability management program
- educate staff about the mission, values, goals, objectives, principles and benefits associated with the disability management program
- maintain contact with the disabled employee and identify suitable work that appropriately accommodates the employee's physical abilities

- provide services or cause services to be provided that will aid in the early and safe return to work of each disabled employee
- review and modify program continually to enhance return-to-work provisions
- solicit and secure relationships with external service providers to reduce the amount of time a disabled employee is off
- establish best practices as they pertain to program design and administration (*i.e.*, does your program take advantage of technological innovations such as electronic forms, case management software?)
- propose program evaluation activities that will aid in the development and improvement of the program

Health care providers (*i.e.*, physician, physiotherapist, occupational therapist) responsibilities:
- optimize the disabled employee's ability to safely return to work in a timely fashion
- assess and make return-to-work recommendations
- gather and incorporate job demands into the rehabilitation of the disabled employee
- safeguard medical information to protect the disabled employee's right to confidentiality
- update stakeholders on the disabled employee's return-to-work program

Union representative responsibilities:
- actively participate in the day-to-day administration of the disability management program (*i.e.*, maintaining contact with the disabled employee)
- promote the principles (*i.e.*, employee well-being) and practices associated with the disability management program
- develop innovative strategies and recommendations for inclusion into a collective bargaining agreement that will promote and further the goals and objectives of the disability management program
- provide support and feedback to the steering committee during program evaluation

SETTING GOALS AND OBJECTIVES

Understanding the issues that positively and negatively impact on your organization's ability to minimize employee absenteeism due to disability is key to ensuring that your disability management program achieves your goals and objectives. To this end, fully assessing your current ability to, first, prevent lost-time claims from occurring and, secondly, facilitate an early and safe return to work of your disabled employees will significantly improve your ability to draft appropriate goals and objectives for your needs.

The following sample goal and objective statements will assist you in developing your own program goals and objectives.

Sample Goal and Objective Statements

Goal

- To help employees stay at work and to encourage an early and safe return following disability or illness.
- To improve communication frequency and information exchange between stakeholders.
- To demonstrate consistency in the management of all employees with disabilities, regardless of cause.

Objectives

- To contact all disabled employees within 24 hours of the onset of the disability.
- To offer suitable work (*i.e.*, work that accommodates the employee's physical abilities) within 48 hours of confirming the disabled employee's fitness for work.
- To maintain contact with the disabled employee at least weekly until the employee has been successfully returned to the labour force.

TIP: *Measure the effectiveness of your objectives by matching them to the following. Each objective should satisfy each of the SMART points.*

S pecific
M easurable
A ttainable
R ealistic
T imed

ESTABLISHING GUIDING PRINCIPLES AND PRACTICES

Guiding principles communicate two things to all stakeholders: the high regard the corporation has for addressing lost time due to disability and the importance the corporation places on returning the employee to work. Guiding principles are not only about following policy and procedures, they help ensure that employees respect the program and its ability to minimize a disability's and/or an illness's impact on an employee.

Guiding principles can be established through ongoing education, communication and evaluation of your staff's ability to meet pre-defined goals and objectives. This may include: the training of supervisors and managers to be more effective communicators; discussing alternative dispute resolution procedures; or having a disabled employee provide supervisors or a steering committee with insight into the physical, emotional and psychological realities of being off work. By continuously improving your disability management program in innovative or creative ways, you will gain and retain the respect of all your employees. This in turn will improve employee motivation, co-operation, loyalty and productivity.

Guiding principle considerations:

- Does management understand the value of addressing your disabled employees' physical, emotional and psychological needs?
- Do your corporate values reflect the notion that "employees are our most important asset"?
- What best practices do you already have in place that could be applied to your disability management program?
- Is program education included in new employee orientation?
- Do previously disabled employees and other internal and external stakeholders have the opportunity to provide feedback?
- Is management's ability to effectively communicate with disabled employees benchmarked and evaluated?
- Are program principles applied equally and company-wide to all disabled employees?
- Is your disability management co-ordinator knowledgeable about the roles and responsibilities of the other stakeholders (*i.e.*, physicians, physiotherapists), return-to-work practices, employee counselling, problem solving, communication techniques, legislative obligations, organizational skills, ethical considerations, meeting skills, labour management relations and program promotion?

Program Promotion and Education

Just as marketing is required to effectively sell a product or service, it is also required to sell and promote your disability management program. The more information you communicate to your employees through newsletters, bulletin boards, e-mail, web sites, orientation manuals, meetings or brochures, the more success you will have in returning your disabled employee to work. The steering committee should play a central role in identifying the most appropriate marketing methodologies and co-ordinating the development of materials like brochures, posters or labour/management presentations.

Program promotion is most effective when it is continuous. To this end beginning the program promotion before the program start date will provide both management and labour with the opportunity to become familiar with the stakeholder benefits and responsibilities before the program is rolled out. Releasing key facts about the program on a regular basis (*i.e.*, monthly) throughout the development process and after the program launch will aid in ensuring all stakeholders are receptive to the program. Once the program is up and running, monthly or quarterly updates on program successes will help keep the program in the forefront of your employees' minds. Always take into account the demographic profile of your workforce. Consider your employees' literacy and language skills, their average age, academic levels and general learning abilities.

Dispute Resolution

For the most part, dispute resolution is a formalized problem-solving mechanism where two parties in dispute, along with an objective third party, identify issues, find common ground and agree to mutually acceptable activities that will mitigate the identified differences.

The mediator facilitates discussion between the parties, usually an employee and an employer, and in so doing assists the employer and employee to understand the other's perspective. Perhaps the most important role the mediator can play is offering settlement ideas that in turn will create a win-win outcome. Mediators have a responsibility to explain their role in making the mediation process work. In addition, mediators have a duty to ensure they conduct a process that provides each party the opportunity to voice their views and concerns.

In dispute resolution, facts and issues are openly communicated in arriving at a mutually agreeable settlement. Both parties in dispute always have the option of not participating in the formal process and crafting a solution on their own.

In the event a solution cannot be found, other options include arbitration or filing an appeal with the appropriate body. For example, if the dispute concerned a workers' compensation claim, the compensation board itself may offer you and your employee dispute resolution services. Getting involved in a dispute resolution process is a no-lose situation. The worst-case scenario is the mediation process does not remedy the situation.

Discussion between the parties remains confidential with the exception of information that can be interpreted as contrary to legislation or policy or documentation that has been previously discussed and released. If a mutually satisfactory agreement is reached the mediator will document that fact and include a brief explanation of agreement details.

Listed below is a sample dispute resolution policy and procedure statement.

Sample Dispute Resolution Policy

The (company) maintains an open door policy. All employees will be treated fairly, justly and equitably. The company will act immediately should problems occur. All employees are encouraged to bring forward to management any complaints or recommendations dealing with the disability management program without fear of reprisal.

Any disputes, controversies, or suggestions must first be handled between the employee and supervisor.

An employee who has not obtained a solution within five business days of the circumstances has the right to bring the situation to the attention of the supervisor's immediate supervisor or human resources representative. That person will review the circumstances within five days. Complaints should be documented and include all the relevant facts. The employee and supervisor will receive a response within five more business days.

If the employee remains dissatisfied with the outcome, he or she has the right to discuss the problem with senior management. If the problem cannot be resolved at this level, then the matter can be submitted in writing to the board of directors. Their decision will be final.

PROGRAM EVALUATION

Ensuring that there is a program evaluation component to your disability management program is the only objective way of determining whether your program is accomplishing the intended goals. To this end, having carefully worded goals and objectives will help you immensely. Table 6-1 lists the most common evaluation measures, they can be customized to meet your specific needs.

Table 6-1 - Sample Evaluation Measures

General Program Evaluation		
• Employee absenteeism rate before program implementation		
• Average days off per employee per month/quarter/ year		
• Number of employees absent due to disability or illness		
Stakeholder Perceptions	Yes	No
• Did the disabled employee receive the information required to facilitate an early and safe return to work?		
• Did the attending physician receive an early and safe return-to-work information package?		
• Did your physiotherapist (if required) tailor your treatment program to the physical demands of the job identified on your return-to-work plan?		
External Service Providers' Considerations		
• Did the disabled employees receive the necessary care quickly and timely?		
• Did the treatment providers demonstrate appropriate professionalism in their dealings with disabled employees and other stakeholders (*i.e.*, case manager)?		
• Did the service provider attend to special needs as requested by the case manager, disabled employee or other stakeholder?		
• Did the written documentation, if any, adequately address the information requested?		

	Yes	No
• Was the provider's location reasonably accessible to the employee's residence?		
• Does the provider offer value-added services such as information sessions, automated referral or convenient access to professionals?		

CONFIDENTIALITY

Personal information cannot be released without the prior written consent of the disabled employee. Employee medical information should be accessible only for the purpose of facilitating a return to work.

Information employers need:
- employee functional abilities information
- hours employee can work per day
- estimated return-to-work date
- prognosis
- treatment activities (*i.e.*, therapy, medication frequency)
- capacity to travel to and from work
- return-to-work obstacles
- date employee will be able to resume normal duties (if applicable)
- treatment facility information (contact person, address, rationale for referral, referral date and visitation frequency)

Information employers do not need:
- diagnosis
- treatment history prior to injury
- detailed medical reports
- insurance documentation

SUMMARY

- Stakeholder buy-in should be obtained from the beginning and prompted throughout the design and implementation phases of the program.

- An audit of your current disability management practices will assist you in assessing what works well and what needs to be improved.
- A mission statement should encapsulate the essence of what your company stands for both in the management of employee disability and the importance you place on keeping your employees happy and healthy.
- The steering committee should play a central role in the development and overall management of the program.
- The steering committee should consist of a previously disabled employee, a disability management co-ordinator, health care provider and union representative, if unionized.
- Goals and objectives should reflect your desire to prevent lost-time claims from happening and should ensure appropriate and timely steps are taken to return your disabled employees to work.
- Objectives should be specific, measurable, attainable, realistic and timed (SMART).
- The focus of guiding principles is not just on following policy and procedures, but also on ensuring employees respect the program and its ability to maximize employee wellness.
- Program promotion and education should be regular and continuous.
- Dispute resolution allows the open communication of facts and issues in arriving at a mutually agreeable settlement. A dispute resolution process should be included in your disability management policy and procedures.
- Program evaluation is the only effective way of determining whether your program goals and objectives are being realized. The evaluation should include the views and opinions of both internal and external stakeholders.
- Employee confidentiality should always be paramount in the management of a claim file. The employee *must* be privy to the fact that you, as the employer, are sharing medical information with other stakeholders.

REVIEW QUESTIONS

1. Identify five factors that will affect your ability to gain buy-in from all stakeholders.
2. List 10 issues that will influence the design of your disability management program.
3. Write a mission statement.

4. Define confidentiality and write an action plan to ensure all program stakeholders understand their responsibilities as they pertain to obtaining and releasing confidential information.

CHAPTER 7

Frequently Asked Questions

This chapter addresses some of the most commonly asked questions various stakeholders have concerning the design and implementation of a program. The chapter for the most part is structured around the questions the disability management co-ordinator would receive from a steering committee member, an employee, a manager or external service providers.

This chapter will cover information discussed throughout the book. It will reinforce many of the issues stakeholders will need to consider when designing and implementing a disability management program.

UPPER MANAGEMENT QUESTIONS

Q: Why should we invest time and money in a disability management program?
A: Preventing and proactively managing lost-time claims reduces turn-over, overtime expenses and training and insurance costs and increases employee morale and productivity and labour/management communication. It is estimated that for every $1 a company invests in the prevention and management of employee disability that $5 to $6 is saved.

Investing time and money into programs that enhance your employees' quality of life will positively impact the mission, values and objectives of your company.

Q: What are the costs of starting and running a disability management program?
A: The following budget items address most, if not all, of the costs associated with designing, implementing and running a disability management

program. Actual costs will vary according to the size of your organization, claim frequency, plant locations and organizational considerations.

- human resources (secretarial staff, case manager)
- administration (postage, office equipment)
- marketing (printing)
- insurance premiums (WSIB, STD, LTD)
- education (rental fees, photocopying)
- professional development (conferences, seminars, subscriptions)
- travel (committee member automobile, air or train travel)
- meetings (steering committee meetings)
- consultant or external service provider expenses (*i.e.*, disability management co-ordinator, independent medical evaluation, Functional Abilities Evaluation costs)

Allocating dollars to the program budget is the responsibility of the steering committee. Decisions such as whether or not the disability management co-ordinator is an employee or an external service provider and policies on when to use an independent medical assessment or frequency of marketing and training initiatives will affect the overall costs of implementing and running the program.

Stakeholders influence the policies and procedures of the program; they also shape the budget. Drafting a detailed letter of intent with which all stakeholders are comfortable, will assist in ensuring budgeting is fair and equitable. Use past expenses/budgets to establish cost projections. For example, if in the past you spent $10,000 on legal costs associated with challenging claims, this cost may be significantly reduced based on your new commitment to maintain open communication with your disabled employees and work with them in achieving an early and safe return to work.

Q: When will the company realize cost savings as a result of the disability management program?
A: Implementing a disability management program is largely about making the health and safety of your employees a priority within your organizational culture. By demonstrating a proactive approach to addressing the health and safety needs of your employees you are demonstrating to them that the organization values and cherishes their contributions to the organization's goals. Since in most instances establishing this type of cul-

ture takes time, realizing the full potential of a disability management program can take years.

This is not to say that short-term cost savings are not likely. Savings in the first year of the program, depending on the organization's ability to follow through on the policy and procedures established by the steering committee, are very likely. Short-term cost savings will occur in reduced overtime, recruiting costs and improved productivity. Long-term cost savings such as reduced insurance premiums, workers' compensation costs/surcharges, improved employee morale, and labour/management relations should begin to occur approximately one to three years after program implementation.

Q: How do we attain buy-in from the union?
A: First, the union will need to understand how a disability management program would benefit the union and the employees. Also the union will need a rationale for why it should be involved in the design and ongoing management of the program. It should be pointed out that the disability management program would enhance employee wellness and in turn reduce employee absenteeism and associated costs. Indeed, the union's participation in the program will assist in ensuring disabled employees receive the necessary care and support they require to return to work. Discussion should also include the importance of ensuring that all the stakeholders, especially the disabled employee, view the program as one that both management and labour support. If the union is committed to the program, chances are disabled employees will feel much more comfortable committing to it.

For some, past labour/management relations will impact on future relations. In moving from an adversarial relationship to a co-operative one, it may be difficult to bury feelings of distrust and bitterness. For some, management's invitation to the union to participate in the design and development of the disability management program can, in and of itself, demonstrate management's desire to move towards a relationship that recognizes the value of working co-operatively.

Presenting the program in a way that highlights the issues both union and management have in common will promote discussion that will enhance trust and co-operation. Listed below are some of the priorities that both unions and management value and which can be used to develop and shape your disability management program:

- heath and wellness of employees
- minimization and prevention of employee absenteeism

- education and personal development of employees' skills and abilities

Q: What steps can be taken to gain stakeholder buy-in?

A: Ongoing two-way communication, commitment and co-operation from all stakeholders is required to gain a healthy level of buy-in. All activities that take the three C's into consideration will facilitate buy-in.

Listed below are a number of initiatives and ideas that will assist you in implementing the three C's.

- regular stakeholder meetings (*i.e.*, steering committee meetings with both internal and external service providers)
- written documentation outlining program objectives, benefits organized by stakeholder, roles and responsibilities of each stakeholder, eligibility criteria
- social events (*i.e.*, plant tours for external service providers such as physicians, independent medical providers, physiotherapists)
- surveys for internal and external stakeholders (department heads, employees, supervisors)
- lunch-and-learn education sessions

Q: Will the program assist in preventing lost-time claims?

A: While accident prevention both at and away from work is always the most desirous outcome, it is reasonable to conclude that sooner or later employee absenteeism will occur as a result of disability. The disability management program will assist your organization in two core areas: first, by creating and/or enhancing a health and wellness culture within your organization and secondly, facilitating an early and safe return to work of disabled employees.

Establishing a culture that encourages employees to think about safety in performing their daily activities is always a win-win scenario from both a cost perspective and a physical and emotional health perspective. The more time a company spends promoting health and wellness, the happier the employees will be and the more productive they will be.

Q: How will supervisors, managers and employees be educated about their responsibilities in the program?

A: Educating supervisors, managers and employees about the disability management program and their individual responsibilities usually requires a two-phase approach. Phase one should consist of information seminars,

128

brochures, company-wide or departmental meetings, e-mail correspondence, newsletter articles or inserts and any other mediums your company uses to communicate new information. This should be organized to begin before the program start date so as to facilitate enthusiasm and discussion about how the program will affect the various stakeholders. Phase one should take into account the following: ensure all staff have a good understanding of *why* the disability management program is required, *who* will be involved in the program, *what* the program objectives are, *when* the program will begin and *how* the program will enhance employee health and wellness.

Phase two of the program, or the maintenance phase, will ensure all staff (supervisors, managers and employees) have up-to-date information about the program's successes and changes. It should have clearly defined goals and objectives that ensure information is being disseminated year-round. This may include reporting statistical information such as the average number of lost-time days per claim or average cost per claim as compared to previous years or quarters. Policy changes, new procedures and changes to steering committee representatives should also be reported.

Managerial orientation and training should include:

- legal obligations including workers' compensation and human rights legislation
- interviewing and assessment skills
- early and safe return to work and case management skills
- overview of forms
- negotiation skills
- mediation skills
- preserving confidentiality
- labour/management relations
- time management

Q: How often will the program be evaluated?
A: Ongoing evaluation is really the only objective way of knowing what aspects of your program are working and what aspects need reviewing. It is therefore crucial that the steering committee establish evaluation guidelines and policy. Depending on the size of your organization you may want to establish a list of items that are reviewed quarterly and another list that is evaluated annually. Clearly, the more time you spend addressing the day-to-day problems and issues, the more likely you will be in having program successes both in the short and long term.

Q: What are we currently doing to return disabled employees to work? Why do we need to change it?
A: For many organizations the management of occupational claims (*i.e.*, workers' compensation claims) is much different that non-occupational (*i.e.*, short and long-term disability, motor vehicle accident) claims. Increasingly, employers are recognizing that the origin of the claim or legislative obligations, while important, should not be the driving force behind the company's decision to demonstrate equity among all disabled employees regardless of where or how they became disabled. By managing all lost-time claims in a fair and consistent manner, absenteeism costs are reduced and employee loyalty increases.

Q: Will the program affect the collective bargaining agreement?
A: Your disability management program is about corporate values and principles, doing what is best for the employees and the corporation. If a corporation truly believes in the synergy of its people, the collective bargaining agreement should reflect that. It is therefore reasonable to conclude that the protocols and policies outlined in the collective bargaining agreement will also apply to the terms and conditions associated with the disability management program. There should be no distinguishing rights or privileges between documents.

Q: What qualifications or skills should the disability management co-ordinator possess to develop and implement a disability management program?
A: In 1999, the National Institute of Disability Management and Research ("NIDMAR") developed a document outlining the skills and abilities disability management professionals should possess. NIDMAR identified the following as essential skills and competencies:[1]

- Demonstrate Knowledge of Disability Management Theory and Practice
- Apply Legislation and Benefit Programs
- Labour/Management Relations
- Utilize Communication and Problem-Solving Skills
- Disability Case Management
- Return-to-Work Coordination

---

[1] National Institute of Disability Management, *Occupational Standards in Disability Management*, D. Shrey, ed. (Fort Alberni, B.C., 1999), at pp. 28-33.

- Health, Psychosocial, Prevention, and Functional Aspects of Disability
- Development of Program Management and Evaluation Activities
- Demonstrate Ethical and Professional Conduct

Q: How will my organization determine whether it has the personnel required to assess need and to implement and evaluate a disability management program?
A: Determining what your program's human resources needs are will depend on a number of variables. Listed below are a number of considerations that should be considered by your steering committee:

- disability management program organizational chart
- number of plants
- labour/management relations
- frequency of claims (per month/quarter/year)
- duration of claims (*i.e.*, average number of days, weeks, months an employee is absent)
- nature of disabilities (soft tissue, fractures, amputations, cancer, depression, phobias)
- type of claims (*e.g.*, workers' compensation claims, long-term disability claims)
- rehabilitation services required (*i.e.*, medical or vocational claim management services)
- program objectives

Q: What are our legislative obligations?
A: Disability management programs are governed by two primary pieces of legislation: workers' compensation and human rights.

The objectives of workers' compensation legislation are to promote health and safety in the workplace and to facilitate an early and safe return to work of disabled employees. To this end, provincial governments have increasingly placed more responsibility on the primary stakeholders, particularly the employee and the employer. In Ontario, for example, employers are obligated to maintain ongoing contact with the employee from the onset of disability until returning to work. In addition, employers are obligated to identify work that is within the employee's physical abilities. Likewise, employees are required to provide functional abilities information to their employers and maintain regular communication from the onset of disability until the successful return to work.

Human rights legislation provides employees with protection against discrimination pertaining to age, gender, religion, race, marital status, colour, nationality and disability. In the case of a disabled employee, the legislation requires the employer to make a reasonable effort to accommodate the employee's disability thereby minimizing or eliminating obstacles that otherwise would have prevented the employee from performing the essential duties of the job. Employers are required to make accommodation to the point of undue hardship. The courts and the commission have defined undue hardship as an accommodation that exceeds an employer's financial resources, or that would result in bankruptcy.

There are other laws that also impact on the management of your disabled employees such as the *Occupational Health and Safety Act* (Ontario)[2] and confidentiality legislation. For more detailed information about the legislation mentioned please visit your provincial government's web site.

Q: Who determines if workstation modifications are cost feasible?

A: Workplace parties control modifications. In the event the workplace parties cannot agree on what is reasonable, the matter can be referred — in the case of a workers' compensation claim — to your workers' compensation board for assistance in identifying which modifications are essential and which are not. If agreement cannot be obtained after the workers' compensation board's ergonomist has made recommendations, the matter can be referred to a human rights commission for investigation. Keep in mind that the costs associated with going beyond the company level can be *significant*. It is always in the best interests of all parties to attempt to work through the issues without bringing in external parties.

Some workers' compensation boards provide mediation services to assist employers and employees in resolving differences and in expediting a worker's return to work. Please contact your workers' compensation board for more information about this.

A number of private organizations exist in various communities that will provide ergonomic assessments, workstation modification recommendations and educational services pertaining to work accommodations and end-user training. These services can be found via the Yellow Pages, web site searches, word of mouth or trade magazine advertising.

---

[2] R.S.O. 1990, c. O.1.

EMPLOYEE QUESTIONS

Q: What is a disability management program?

A: Following the onset of a disability whether it is work-related or not, you and the company along with other stakeholders develop a plan of action that will address most, if not all, of the issues preventing you from returning to work. The program considers a number of return-to-work possibilities beginning with your pre-disability job, comparable jobs (other less demanding jobs that require the same skills and abilities) or suitable jobs (other less demanding jobs, with different skill requirements). Every effort is made to modify your pre-disability job to ensure your abilities match the requirements of the job. Modified work, workstation accommodation and graduated return-to-work programs are always considered.

Q: How will a disability management program benefit me?

A: The disability management program promotes regular communication between employer and employee. This ensures that your needs are being addressed quickly and appropriately. In the past little or no communication occurred between the employer and employee, resulting in inaccurate assumptions being made by both parties about return-to-work potential. By maintaining ongoing communication, crucial information such as job demands and return-to-work obstacles can be shared between the case manager and external service providers, thus ensuring that the information each stakeholder is relaying is enhancing your recovery. For example, when a physiotherapist designs a treatment program to restore an employee's level of functioning to the pre-disability level, often the information she relies on is only partial. Detailed work demands such as lifting, carrying and walking activities are estimated. Without a detailed job description that outlines maximum lifting, carrying and walking requirements, the probability of the treatment program restoring the employee's ability to work is unlikely. Conversely, an employer with a formalized disability management program will have the procedures and forms necessary to communicate information when and as required.

Q: What safeguards are available to ensure I'm not forced into a job I'm not comfortable with?

A: Open communication is key to ensuring that issues are addressed. By talking to your supervisor or manager about your abilities, appropriate job matching will occur. It is also important to report ongoing progress or lack

133

of progress both formally and informally to your case manager regularly. Addressing your needs is crucial to a successful outcome.

If, for any reason the return-to-work plan has been unsuccessful in facilitating your return to work, the steering committee and other providers will assess the facts of the case and make recommendations.

Q: How do I qualify for the program?
A: Any employee who is unable to work due to disability or illness is eligible to participate in the program. You remain eligible until one of the following occur: all possible job options have been exhausted within the company, or you reach the age of retirement.

Q: What are my responsibilities after I become disabled?
A: Once it has been determined that you are unable to work as a result of a disability or illness you will be responsible for the following:

- contacting your supervisor to report your disability
- completing a functional abilities form with your family physician
- meeting with your case manager to assess your return-to-work needs
- attending to recommended treatment and/or assessments as agreed to by you, your physician, your employer and other stakeholders (*e.g.*, insurance carrier)
- maintaining weekly contact with your case manager or co-ordinator
- identifying work that is within your abilities
- participating in the design and implementation of the return-to-work plan
- participating in follow-up meetings to discuss your progress and return-to-work needs

Q: What can I expect from my employer?
A: Like you, your employer plays an important role in ensuring you enjoy a safe and early return to work. Your employer, through the steering committee, will make available resources and job options that will assist you in returning to work.

Following a report of an absent employee due to disability or illness your supervisor or a designate will:

- provide you with an information brochure that will explain the disability management program and your responsibilities
- provide you with forms (*i.e.*, Return to Work Functional Abilities Information, see Form 5 of the Appendix) that will assist in matching your physical abilities to an appropriate job
- maintain ongoing contact with you and the other stakeholders through telephone calls and meetings to discuss your return-to-work needs
- develop in consultation with you and the other stakeholders a return-to-work plan
- consult with internal and external disability management specialists to clarify your medical needs, employability, job accommodation and workstation design
- provide various administrative services that will facilitate your early and safe return to work

By working together, you and your employer can create a win-win scenario that in turn will make the company more competitive.

Q: What happens if I am unable to return to my regular job due to my disability?
A: During the assessment, treatment and return-to-work phases of your rehabilitation, your manager and rehabilitation professionals will be evaluating your ability to return to your regular job in the first instance, secondly to a comparable job — a job that is comparable in skills, responsibilities and wage to your regular job — and thirdly, to a job that is within your physical abilities and takes advantage of the skills you have gained through your work experience and which maximizes your earnings potential.

Through the rehabilitation period your employer and/or the designated rehabilitation professional will discuss the various job options available to you. Your ability to return to work will depend on a number of variables including the seriousness of your disability, your prognosis for recovery, job availability, job location, work hours, job responsibilities, your ability to learn new information or complete formal training or on-the-job training.

Occasionally, due to a number of intervening variables, your employer is unable to identify a job that will accommodate your needs. In this scenario a workers' compensation board or a private insurance carrier will assume responsibility for assisting you in identifying alternate job options and returning to work with another employer.

Q: What rights do I have that will assist me in returning to meaningful work?

A: Disabled employees have a number of rights as they pertain to minimizing the impact a disability may have on their ability to work. The two pieces of legislation that govern your rights are human rights and workers' compensation. These Acts are controlled and developed by provincial governments, they therefore differ from province to province. For example, a workplace accident that occurs in Ontario would be subject to workers' compensation legislation in Ontario (*Workplace Safety and Insurance Act, 1997*[3]). A workplace accident in British Columbia would need to conform to the various sections outlined in the *Workers Compensation Act*[4] of British Columbia.

Human rights legislation requires employers to provide accommodation to assist disabled employees return to meaningful work. For example, if a disabled employee's impairment prevented him from performing an essential duty of his job, the employer is required by law to accommodate that job to match the employee's abilities. Generally speaking, the only limitation precluding an employer from accommodating the employee's needs at a Human Rights Commission hearing would be if the employer could demonstrate that the accommodation would cause undue hardship. This is generally accepted to mean that the accommodation would result in significant financial hardship to the employer.

Q: Is participation in the program voluntary?

A: The disability management program is designed to create a win-win scenario. It is therefore advantageous for both the disabled employee and the employer to participate in the program.

Your employer has invested a great deal of time and money into designing, implementing and managing the program, they believe that the time and money invested makes good business sense for both the employer and the employee. In most cases the program will reduce the length of time you are off work due to disability and in turn will improve your quality of life both at and away from work.

By not participating in the program, you increase the chance of not returning to work either with your current employer or another employer. In addition, lack of co-operation may negatively impact your ability to

---

[3]   S.O. 1997, c. 16, Sch. A.

[4]   R.S.B.C. 1996, c. 492.

receive income replacement benefits. This is assessed on a case-by-case basis.

Q: What happens if I disagree with the rehabilitation plan?
A: Paramount to the design and development of the rehabilitation plan is ongoing communication and co-operation. The rehabilitation plan is a culmination of many activities including a disability assessment and information sharing and is based on the belief that by working together a positive outcome will be realized by all. All parties or stakeholders have an equal say in what is required to ensure the employee enjoys an early and safe return to work. Respect for each stakeholder must be demonstrated throughout the process.

Various formal and informal measures are available when a dispute arises. The disability management program should have a dispute resolution process in place before a dispute arises. The employer and disabled employee must agree to refer the dispute to the steering committee for a non-binding recommendation and resolution. If, for any reason, the employee or employer representatives are unhappy with the recommendation, a neutral third party arbitrator is appointed to resolve the matter. A list of third party arbitrators should be available to both parties before the dispute arises so as to ensure both parties are aware of the options available to them.

None of the above scenarios prevent other initiatives from occurring. For example, the Ontario Workplace Safety and Insurance Board provides no fee dispute mediation services to assist parties in resolving disputes. The mediator assists the parties in developing a plan to which both the employee and the employer can agree. The recommendations are not binding, but in many cases result in a desirable outcome. This service is only provided for workers' compensation claims.

Q: Am I eligible for the program if I become disabled away from work?
A: In many organizations, the answer is yes.

In the past, many employers were only concerned about workers' compensation claims. They reasoned that if they managed their workers' compensation claim effectively, their costs would be contained.

With changes to health care legislation, short and long-term disability costs have significantly increased. Recognizing that non-occupational disability costs are also significant, most employers have realized the importance of proactively managing all disability claims regardless of where the disability occurred.

Q: What role will the union play in the management of my disability?
A: The union has a central role in the design, implementation and management of the disability management program. It can be a valuable ally in assisting both employees and management to address specific issues that can reduce the length of time an employee is off work. In addition, the union can act as a facilitator in educating employees about program benefits. More so than ever, unions offer a plethora of knowledge and skills that can be used to benefit all stakeholders.

The union can act as a resource in providing information and direction. While the rehabilitation professional is the primary manager of your case, the union representative can reinforce information shared at an employee/employer meeting or provide the necessary impetus for you to feel confident about raising an issue. The union is there to support you in your efforts to return to work whether through moral support or otherwise. Its support will enhance your understanding and acceptance of the program.

Q: Who is involved in determining when I am ready to return to work?
A: Determining your ability to work is dependent on a number of stakeholders: you, your employer, your physician, your health care provider, the insurance representative and a case manager. Due to the various dynamics associated with your claim, all of these people play a significant role in ensuring that your return to work is medically appropriate and safe. Each of these players will have some input into the decision.

In most cases your health care provider and/or your physician will be asked to complete a form that will outline your physical abilities and your treatment needs. This form will provide the detailed information your employer requires to match your abilities to a job. Depending on the completeness of the form your employer may also contact your health care provider or physician to obtain clarification or a medical opinion. Your employer will always ask for your consent prior to contacting an external service provider.

When all parties agree that a return to work is possible, a meeting with you, your supervisor and/or case manager will be arranged to assess various job options and to design and implement a return-to-work plan. All stakeholders sign the plan. The stakeholder signatures demonstrate their willingness to agree to the objectives and activities outlined on the plan. If the plan requires changes, a new plan is created with signatures.

After you return to work, regular follow-up meetings will occur to ensure you are continuing to make progress. If problems develop, the appropriate stakeholder or service provider will be contacted for further consultation and discussion.

Q: During my graduated return-to-work program, will my productivity be used to evaluate my rate of progress?
A: No. A graduated return-to-work program is required to improve your ability to work full-time hours. It is usually required when an employee has been off work for a lengthy period of time (*i.e.*, one month or more). The graduated hours allow the employee to build up endurance and strength that have been lost during a period of lost time. The more physically demanding a job is, the more beneficial graduated hours will be. For example, if your job requires you to lift 50 pounds repetitively, a graduated hours program could be used to build up your arm, leg and back strength. Graduated hours can also reduce the probability of further injury or aggravation.

Graduated work hours can also be used as a form of treatment. In some instances the treatment provider is unable to simulate a job demand (*e.g.*, lifting 50 pounds repetitively). The treatment centre would therefore work with you to improve your lifting abilities to say 25 pounds and the workplace would be used to restore your lifting capacity to the required 50 pounds. This is not always possible but can be quite effective when implemented.

STEERING COMMITTEE QUESTIONS

Q: How will disputes be handled?
A: Disputes occur from time to time. It is therefore important to have a dispute procedure designed and agreed to before the disability management program commences. A dispute mechanism policy should include the following:

- a list of mediators who can be reached in short order to mediate a dispute
- clear documentation about when the dispute mechanism should be used

- checks and balances to ensure impartiality is maintained throughout the process
- checks and balances to avoid conflicts of interest
- a mediator who is experienced in providing mediation services in your area of need (*e.g.*, if the issue in dispute concerns return to work, the mediator should be experienced in return-to-work mediation)
- clear documentation covering what circumstances need to exist to terminate or suspend the mediation process

Q: Who will be invited to sit on the steering committee?

A: The steering committee should be a blend of all those individuals who directly or indirectly play a role in the early and safe return to work of disabled employees within your organization. This will include upper, middle and lower management, line staff, the union (if applicable) and internal service providers, such as an occupational health nurse or physician. Ideally, the line staff representative should be familiar with the issues that a disabled employee would experience.

In addition to the internal staff, external providers should also be encouraged to participate. This may include family physicians, health care providers such as physiotherapists, psychologists, disability management specialists, workers' compensation and insurance carrier representatives.

All these stakeholders will add value and significance to the overall effectiveness of the steering committee's ability to design a program that will meet the needs of employees and the corporation.

Q: How will committee members be selected?

A: The steering committee plays an important role in the design and development of the disability management program. Having members who can communicate and demonstrate the values associated with facilitating disabled employees back to work is crucial.

While every program has a number of common characteristics, special attention should be paid to acquiring members who understand the uniqueness of your organization. Having the ability to gain buy-in from the other stakeholders by relating to that individual's priorities, values and principles is a skill in itself. By having prior relations with the various stakeholders, the committee will be in a better position to determine the most synergistic people for the committee. Synergy, while important, should not override the need for skilled and experienced committee members. Committee members should possess the following skills:

- an ability to understand the issues a disabled employee may endure during the disability
- an understanding of the direct and indirect costs associated with employee disability
- an understanding of the impact a disability management program will have on all stakeholders
- an understanding of the organization's values, principles and objectives
- an openness to new ideas, concepts and changes that will positively impact *all* stakeholders
- an understanding of the administrative and legislative requirements to develop, implement, manage and evaluate the disability management program
- respect of the individuals being represented
- respect of the other stakeholders both inside and outside the organization

Q: What are the committee's responsibilities?

A: The committee is responsible for the overall design, implementation and evaluation of the program. Depending on the structure of your committee, it may also be involved in resolving claim disputes. Some steering committees will opt to have preferred external service providers that will provide specific services such as Functional Abilities Evaluations or independent medical evaluations. If this were the case, the committee would be responsible for negotiating contracts with the various providers. Listed below are a number of other steering committee responsibilities:

- ongoing program marketing and stakeholder education
- formulating objectives, policies and procedures including dispute resolution
- selecting disability management co-ordinator(s) and other committee members
- problem-solving administrative deficiencies
- developing and customizing best practices
- program implementation and evaluation
- ensuring consistency
- maintaining positive relations with disabled employees and internal and external service providers through planned activities throughout the year (*i.e.*, open house for external service providers, newsletters or other social events)

- making available non-confidential documentation to management and other stakeholders (*e.g.*, statistical information)
- steering committee member performance reviews
- formal and informal training for committee members including applicable legislation, insurance policy terms and benefits, evaluation techniques, early and safe return-to-work principles and practices, occupational health and safety practices, roles and responsibilities of disability management professionals (*e.g.*, occupational nurse, disability management co-ordinator, kinesiologist)

Q: When will the program begin?

A: Most employers have some process in place either formally or informally to return their disabled employees to work. As a result, some or all of the issues that need to be addressed prior to launching the program can be covered in a relatively short period of time. For employers with informal programs, the activities required to formalize their programs may be a matter of writing procedures based on what has been occurring already. For other organizations the existing program may need to be abandoned and a new one developed from scratch. A thorough needs assessment should be completed; it will assist the steering committee in making decisions about what the best course of action would be.

Once it is determined what will be required, a formalized action plan can be developed that will scope out what, when, how, why and where activities must take place. An appropriate start date can be derived from the implementation action plan.

Q: How many committee members will we need?

A: The number of members you recruit for your committee will be largely dependent on the size of your organization. For example, a corporation of 10,000 employees may require several committees to effectively run the program, while a company with 100 employees may only require four members depending on the committee's responsibilities.

At a minimum the steering committee should consist of:

- one disability management co-ordinator
- one senior manager or vice president
- one employee (ideally an employee who has lost time due to disability)
- one union representative

142

Both management and labour should have equal representation on the committee.

Q: How will we recruit and retain committee members?
A: Most organizations have employees who are always looking to develop their skills and abilities. This is such an opportunity. In addition to skill development, committee members will also enjoy the opportunity to participate in meetings during their shift and have the opportunity to contribute to a program that either they or a colleague may require in the future.

Committee membership should be limited to a three-year term unless otherwise agreed to by all the committee members. This will give other interested parties the opportunity to become involved.

The incentives listed below can be used to recruit and retain committee members when interest or participation is problematic. If you are offering these incentives to one member, they should be offered to all committee members:

- free formal and informal training programs
- participation in various out-of-plant tours (*i.e.*, treatment centres or plant visits as a means of developing best practices)
- participation in seminars and/or conferences

Q: How will seniority be protected when determining alternate jobs for disabled employees?
A: There are no hard and fast rules when determining whether or not employee seniority has been affected as a result of a modified work program or placement of an employee into another job that accommodates his or her needs. This is a matter that will require the input of individuals from union (if applicable) and management. When considering the fairness or equity of placing a disabled employee into an alternate position, consider whether or not the placement is long or short term or permanent. In many scenarios, this will be the essential issue in dispute. Always consider the fact that modified work for the most part is a tool used to help an employee get back to his or her regular job. If it is determined that the employee will not be returning to his or her regular job as a result of a disability then alternate jobs that reflect the employee's experience, skills, earnings and learning potential should be considered. For example, if an employee was a machine operator and it was determined that the pre-disability job would not be suitable, the following job solutions would be considered, in order:

- job modifications
- other machine operator positions
- other comparable positions within, then outside that bargaining group
- occupations outside the organization

When balancing the seniority issues to ensure equality is had by all, it is also important to consider the legislative obligations by which employers need to abide. In the case of a non-occupational disability, human rights legislation (duty to accommodate) applies. In the case of an occupational disability, workers' compensation legislation applies. This is not to imply that human rights legislation does not apply to a workers' compensation claim, but rather, other obligations above and beyond human rights legislation must be considered. For example, in the case of the Ontario *Workplace Safety and Insurance Act*, employers are obligated to maintain contact with their disabled employees throughout the period of disability and offer them work that is consistent with their physical abilities. Re-employment obligations also apply in some cases.

The legislation discussed above supersedes collective bargaining agreement provisions pertaining to accommodating disabled employees.

Q: Will return-to-work policies and procedures for non-occupational claims be handled the same way as occupational claims?
A: Managing employee disability is not about conforming to legislative obligations, rather it is a means of maximizing the skills and abilities of your most valuable and expensive assets. With that in mind, it would be unreasonable to conclude that an employee injured and disabled at work requires or deserves more case management or attention than an employee injured and disabled away from work. The skills and abilities of both employees are equally important in ensuring a product or service is delivered.

For those reasons, all disabled employees, regardless of disability origin, should be handled equally. By demonstrating your commitment (through best practices) to returning all your disabled employees to work, legislative consideration will become a non-issue.

Q: How will service providers be selected and evaluated?
A: In completing your needs analysis it will become clear which needs can be filled internally and which needs will require external specialization. With research you will acquaint yourself with a number of service providers who will assist you in making your program the best it can be.

If your steering committee opts to develop formalized agreements with external service providers, the following issues need to be considered:

- What service need will the provider(s) fill?
- How often will the service be required?
- What capabilities and competencies from a human resources perspective and an administrative perspective does the provider have in place?
- How and where will the service be provided?
- Under what conditions can the contract be terminated or extended?
- What are the payment terms?
- What are the liability responsibilities?
- Dispute resolution?
- Confidentiality issues?
- How and when will you communicate with the provider?

Q: What role will the committee play in actually returning the disabled employee to work?

A: The primary role of the steering committee is to generally oversee the program and specifically monitor the process, stakeholder responsibilities, promotion and evaluation. The committee does not play an active role in returning disabled employees to work. Conversely, the disability management co-ordinator is integral in returning employees to work. The co-ordinator, unless otherwise assigned, meets with the disabled employee to complete a needs assessment, the physician to share information and obtain medical information, and the supervisor to obtain an accurate understanding of the employee's job responsibilities. The co-ordinator also facilitates a return to work through ongoing contact with internal and external stakeholders and addresses obstacles on a case-by-case basis.

Q: Will the committee have access to employee medical information and/or other documentation as it pertains to the employee's disability?

A: Issues around confidentiality are usually best handled by applying the need-to-know principle. For example, if the steering committee was resolving an employee dispute pertaining to physical abilities, it is reasonable to conclude that medical information would be required. The committee would require a release of information signed by the employee. In most cases the committee would not be privy to specific claim file information.

Q: How can the committee gain respect from the other stakeholders?
A: Selecting committee members who have gained the respect of their peers and others will drastically improve your ability to establish credibility early on and throughout the implementation of the program. For this reason, special consideration needs to be given to the selection of the steering committee members. The time you spend upfront will significantly improve your ability to enjoy program success in the future.

Ongoing initiatives should be used to reinforce the trust and respect that each of the committee members have achieved. Provision should also be made to remove a committee member who is unable to adequately represent his or her constituency. Electing steering committee members every three years may be an effective way of giving management and labour a means of ensuring the committee members perform. More drastic action may be required if a committee member is in breach of his or her pledge to represent his or her constituents faithfully.

Q: How will the disability management program incorporate services offered by insurance carriers and other providers to make the program more seamless?
A: Determining what your external service provider needs are should occur during the needs assessment phase of your program. Determine what you do well and what needs to be improved. Use external service providers to reduce or eliminate your program weaknesses.

By discussing your intentions to develop a comprehensive disability management program with your current external service providers you will learn about programs and services that are available to you for which you are probably already paying. These may include assessment services or free publications and sample policy wording.

Q: When will independent medical evaluations be used?
A: An independent medical evaluation ("IME") is used to gain insight into a disabled employee's treatment needs, return-to-work obstacles, prognosis and estimated recovery date. An IME gives a second medical opinion while taking into account a number of variables specific to a given claim. Psychologists and orthopedic surgeons are two examples of IME providers. The information provided in an IME can be quite helpful in developing a return-to-work plan.

Since IMEs are expensive, the policy should communicate who, what, when, where and how they should be used. A number of private health care/treatment organizations can provide this service. For the most part, the disability management co-ordinator will determine when or if an IME is appropriate. Depending on the nature of the claim (workers' compensation, short or long-term disability claim) the insurance carrier may fund the IME. Since this may not always be possible, some money should be set aside to fund employer-sponsored IMEs. The policy should include specific questions that can be used by the disability management co-ordinator to determine whether an employer-sponsored IME is appropriate. Questions may include: Have all external service providers been approached to fund the IME? Is the IME required to return the disabled employee to work? What other less expensive options are available (*e.g.*, discussing the claim with the family physician or employer physician)?

Q: When will confidential employee information be provided to external service providers?

A: Without exception employee consent is required to release medical information to all external service providers. This policy should be communicated to *all* committee members and stakeholders. This is a fundamental right of any disabled employee. Information sharing that does not respect this right may result in program disruptions both at a claim level and throughout the organization.

Confidential medical information is valuable to an external service provider. It provides them with insights that otherwise would not be available. It assists them in understanding the issues and return-to-work obstacles. It assists them in strategizing what issues need to be discussed with the disabled employee, the employer and other stakeholders. Generally speaking, the more information you provide, the more background the service provider will have for organizing facts, providing an assessment and drawing conclusions. The assessor is in a better position to determine what information will be helpful. As a result, the assessor should have the opportunity to screen the information he or she feels is significant. Having said that, released medical information should always have a direct relevance to the claim. The steering committee should be consulted if in doubt.

Q: How will providers be evaluated?

A: There are many ways of ensuring that your external service providers maintain a level of service that is required to effectively manage your program. The following items should be considered when formally or informally evaluating your providers:

Timeliness of service:
- Number of days that have elapsed between referral and the employee assessment.
- Number of days that elapse between employee assessment date and the report.
- Did the provider contact you to explain delays or problems?
- Did the provider respond in a timely fashion to questions or concerns by you, the employer or other stakeholders, such as the disabled employee?

Quality of reports:
- Did the report answer the referral questions in an easy-to-understand manner?
- Was the report organized, concise and free of grammatical and spelling errors?
- Were the recommendations supported with good rationale?

Ease of use:
- Is the facility easy to access by public or private transportation?
- Did the disabled employee receive service facility and schedule orientation (washroom location, break times, eating facilities)?
- Is the facility wheelchair accessible?

Q: How will information be exchanged between provider, employer, employee and other stakeholders?
A: With electronic communication becoming increasingly popular, clearly articulating your policy on the ways and means of communicating sensitive and non-sensitive information is essential. The following should be considered:

Internal communication:
- between committee members
- company wide
- inter-departmental
- intra-departmental

External communication:
- with service provider
- with stakeholder (*e.g.*, physician, employee)
- with insurance carriers

If information can be exchanged in a secured environment, meaning that the only individuals who can read the information are those for which it was intended, then electronic communication is a desirable medium. If there is reason to believe that this is not the case, alternative mediums should be used. Your decision to opt in or out of electronic communication will depend on your organization's technological capabilities and priorities.

Appendix

Form 1
RETURN-TO-WORK PLAN

CLIENT NAME & ADDRESS

EMPLOYER NAME & ADDRESS

REHABILITATION PHASE: ☐ PRE-VOCATIONAL ☐ JOB PREPARATION ☐ RETURN-TO-WORK

OBJECTIVE: ☐ RETURN TO PRE-ACCIDENT ☐ RETURN TO COMPARABLE
☐ RETURN TO SUITABLE WORK

Activities	Employer	Employee	Manager	Start Date	End Date

SPECIAL INSTRUCTIONS

This rehabilitation plan is mutually acceptable to all the signatories. It is agreed that through the co-operation of the employer, the employee and the case manager the above objectives will be achieved. All parties agree and understand that this plan may change as required in accordance with the rehabilitation process and in the event of substantial changes will be brought back to all parties for review.

EMPLOYEE _____ EMPLOYER _____

PHYSICIAN _____ CASE MANAGER _____

DATE_____

Form 2
STATUS REPORT

Date:

Employee:
Claim #:
Date of Disability:
Body part:
Service provider contact:

CLAIM MANAGEMENT ACTIVITY SUMMARY:

MANAGER'S IMPRESSIONS:

RECOMMENDATIONS:

1.

2.

3.

Form 3
SAMPLE PHYSICIAN LETTER

Letterhead

Date

Dear [name of family physician]:

Mr./Ms. [employee name] has informed us that he/she is unable to perform the essential duties of his/her job as of [day/month/year].

To assist us in facilitating his/her return to work, we would appreciate your assistance in completing the attached form and returning it to us as soon as possible.

[Company name] is committed to working with you to return [employee name] back to work. By completing the attached Return to Work Functional Abilities Information form, you will assist us in ensuring [employee's name] will have an early and safe return to work.

Thank you for your assistance in this matter, we will be happy to reimburse you up to [dollar amount max: $50] for completion of this form. Please submit an invoice with the completed form.

Sincerely,

[Employer or representative]

APPENDIX

Form 4
PHYSICAL DEMANDS ANALYSIS FORM

Job title:
Pay range:
Evaluator's name:
Date of assessment:
Plant location:
Department:
Supervisor's name and contact number:

JOB OVERVIEW
❑ Primary Responsibilities:
1.

2.

3.

4.

❑ Description of tools, materials and machines:
1.

2.

3.

4.

5.

❑ Normal work hours:
❑ Break and lunch frequency and duration:
❑ Product manufactured or service provided:
❑ Job accommodation available: YES/NO?
WORK ENVIRONMENT
❑ Outside activities: YES/NO? (if yes, see below)
  ■ Is the employee required to work in hot or cold temperatures? YES/NO
  ■ Does the employee have the appropriate lighting? YES/NO
  ■ Is the employee exposed to excessive noise? YES/NO
  ■ Is the employee exposed to ultraviolet light? YES/NO
  ■ Is the employee exposed to poor air quality? YES/NO
  ■ Is the employee exposed to uneven walking surfaces? YES/NO
  ■ Is protective footwear required? YES/NO

WORK ENVIRONMENT CONTINUED

❏ Inside activities? YES/NO? (if yes, see below)
- Is the job located in one primary location? YES/NO
- Does the job require protective clothing? YES/NO
- Are the floors and walkways smooth and clear? YES/NO
- Is protective footwear required? YES/NO

PHYSICAL DEMANDS

❏ Describe all job tasks according to the following physical demands. Include frequency of each task.

> **Example:**
> **Standing:** Continuously; setting, adjusting and repairing machine guides, cutters and loading raw materials
>
> **Frequency Legend:**
> **Continuously:** more than 67% of shift
> **Frequently:** up to 67% of shift
> **Occasionally:** up to 33% of shift
> **Rarely:** up to 10% of shift

- Standing:

- Sitting:

- Squatting:

- Kneeling:

- Walking:

- Bending:

- Stair or ladder climbing:

- Lifting less than 10 lbs.:

- Lifting between 10 lbs. and 35 lbs.:

- Lifting over 35 lbs.:

PHYSICAL DEMANDS CONTINUED
- Reaching:

- Twisting:

- Pushing/Pulling:

- Crawling:

- Handling:

- Carrying less than 10 lbs.:

- Carrying between 10 lbs. and 35 lbs.:

- Carrying over 35 lbs.:

- Grasping:

- Balancing

❑ Job modification considerations
- Is the employee able to change positions? YES/NO
- Can a graduated increase in work hours be considered? YES/NO
- Can the workstation be modified to reduce physical demands? YES/NO
- Is job sharing or job rotation available? YES/NO
- Are adjustable chairs available? YES/NO
- Are lifting and carrying tools available? YES/NO

NOTES

Form 5
RETURN TO WORK FUNCTIONAL ABILITIES INFORMATION

Worker's Name	Date of Injury

Injury

Treatment YES/NO (If YES, please list treatment recommendations with approximate start and end dates)

Frequency Rating: Constantly: > 4 hours; Frequently: 2 to 4 hours; Occasionally: 1 to 2 hours; Rarely: less than 1 hour

Physical Abilities	Maximum Tolerances	Check column that reflects worker's current ability			
		Constantly	Frequently	Occasionally	Rarely
Lifting	lbs				
floor to waist	lbs				
waist to shoulders	lbs				
above shoulders	hrs/min				
Standing	hrs/min				
Walking	hrs/min				
Sitting	hrs/min				
Crouching	hrs/min				
Squatting	hrs/min				
Kneeling	hrs/min				
Gripping	hrs/min				
Fingering	hrs/min				
Bending	hrs/min				
Climbing	hrs/min				
Twisting	hrs/min				
Neck	hrs/min				
Back	hrs/min				
Reaching	hrs/min				
Right Arm	hrs/min				
Left Arm	hrs/min				
Balancing	hrs/min				
Pushing	lbs				
Pulling	lbs				
Carrying	lbs				

Can the worker return to work providing the above-noted tolerances are observed? Please circle YES or NO. If NO, please explain:

Physician's printed name, signature and telephone #   Date of Assessment

Form 6
EMPLOYEE DISABILITY ASSESSMENT

Date

Name
Address
City, Prov.
Postal Code

Employee: Mr. Mrs. Ms.
Claim #:
Date of disability:
Diagnosis:
Date of referral:
Date of birth:
Case manager:
Meeting date:
Occupation:

EXECUTIVE SUMMARY

CLAIMANT MEDICAL HISTORY
[Pre-accident medication, previous injuries, impact on current injury, pre-accident treatment]

SUMMARY OF MEDICAL REPORTS

ACTIVITIES OF DAILY LIVING
Pre- and post-accident:
AM/PM/Weekends
Eating
Sleeping
Entertainment
Exercise
Hobbies
Volunteer
Church
Work
Home making
Inside/outside
Family

EDUCATION HISTORY
[Prov./grade/Subject area]

CERTIFICATES AND LICENCES
[driver's licence/class]

EMPLOYMENT HISTORY

Employer	Job Title	Dates	Responsibilities

PHYSICIAN CONTACT

Employee complaints

Frequency of visits

Physical abilities

Treatment needs

Medication

Pre-existing health

Prognosis

Specialist referrals

Recommendations

WORKSTATION EVALUATION

Pre-accident job assessment (job title, primary tasks and physical demands and frequency rating):

Modified work available (job title, primary tasks, suitability for injured worker):

Physical demands

Rating classifications: Repetitive/Frequently/Occasionally/Rarely
Standing
Sitting
Crouching
Squatting/Stooping
Kneeling
Walking
Bending
Climbing
Lifting $\leq$ 10lbs $\leq$ 20lbs $\leq$ 30lbs $\leq$ 40lbs $\leq$ 50lbs $>$ 50lbs
Floor to table
Table to shoulder
Above shoulder
Carrying
Reaching
Twisting
Pushing/Pulling
Crawling
Handling
Fingering
Grasping
Balancing

EMPLOYEE PERCEPTIONS, PRIORITIES AND MOTIVATION
[statements]

CASE MANAGER IMPRESSIONS
[return-to-work date, obstacles, claimant body language, motivation, living arrangements, physical appearance, personality, communication skills]

CONCLUSIONS/RECOMMENDATIONS

SERVICE PROVIDERS

Treating Physician:
Address:

Telephone:

Fax:

Last contact date:

Physiotherapist:
Address:

Telephone:

Fax:

Last contact date:

Specialist:
Address:

Telephone:

Fax:

Last contact date:

Form 7
TRANSFERABLE SKILLS ANALYSIS

Name:	Employee's Skills Summary
Telephone:	▪
Date of Birth: Age:	▪
Date of Loss:	▪
Claim #:	▪
Address:	▪
	▪
	▪
First Language:	▪
Second Language:	▪
Preferred Work Location:	

Earnings Summary

Job Title	Hourly Rate	Years' Experience
1.	$	
2.	$	
3.	$	
4.	$	
5.	$	
6.	$	

Licences

Name of Licence	Granting Agency	Year Obtained	Currently Active (Yes/No)
1.			
2.			
3.			
4.			
5.			
6.			

Medical History

Body Part	Required Treatment and Dates	Maximum Medical Recovery
		YES/NO
		YES/NO
		YES/NO
		YES/NO
		YES/NO
		YES/NO
		YES/NO
		YES/NO

AN EMPLOYER'S GUIDE TO DISABILITY MANAGEMENT

Physical Restrictions

Activity	Frequency (Constantly, Frequently, Occasionally, Rarely)	Tolerance in lbs. or kg
1.		
2.		
3.		
4.		
5.		
6.		
7.		
8.		
9.		
10.		
11.		

Impressions

1. Is the employee motivated to particiapate in a labour market re-entry program and formalized rehabilitation activities?	Yes/No
2. Does the employee have the necessary stamina to work full time?	Yes/No
3. Is the employee scheduled to participate in further treatment?	Yes/No
4. Is the employee capable of succesfully participating in formal upgrading?	Yes/No
5. Is there anything preventing the employee from returning to work immediately?	Yes/No
6. Has the employee identified any alternative job options?	Yes/No
7. Was the employee healthy prior to the current disability?	Yes/No
8. Does the employee have a good employment history?	Yes/No
9. Is the employee capable of reading, writing and speaking English?	Yes/No
10. Does the employee belong to an association or union?	Yes/No

Skills

Job Title	Skills Required (see National Occupational and Classification Guide)
1.	

APPENDIX

Job Title	Skills Required (see *National Occupational and Classification Guide*)
2.	

Job Title	Skills Required (see *National Occupational and Classification Guide*)
3.	

Job Title	Skills Required (see *National Occupational and Classification Guide*)
4.	

Education

Name of Institution	Country/Province/City	Grade, Diploma, Apprenticeship	Number of Years	Year Completed

Hobbies/Interests (paid and unpaid)

Description of Activity	Years' Experience
1.	
2.	
3.	
4.	
5.	

Comments/Notes

Glossary

accommodation: one or more activities usually performed by the employer to match a job to an employee's physical abilities.

any occupation: a long-term disability insurance policy term. After a period of time, usually two years, an insurance company will consider terminating income replacement benefits unless the employee is unable to perform any occupation that is consistent with his or her skills and experience. *See also* **own occupation**.

assessment: a personal interview with the disabled employee and/or attending physician and possibly other stakeholders as a means of collecting data that will assist in returning the disabled employee to work.

Canadian Association of Rehabilitation Professionals (CARP): a national association that educates, accredits and speaks on behalf of rehabilitation professionals — such as vocational rehabilitation and disability management specialists — to government bodies and others to promote rehabilitation best practices across Canada.

case management: any activity that assists an individual in resuming daily activities. In the case of disability case management, ensuring the disabled employee is physically, emotionally and psychologically fit to resume his or her activities of daily living such as working.

compensable: a workers' compensation or LTD claim for which income replacement benefits and/or rehabilitation benefits are payable by the insurance company. *See also* **non-compensable injury**.

disability: an inability to perform essential activities of daily living such as lifting, bending, walking, standing, gripping and reaching.

disability management: in the broadest sense it is the design, implementation and management of all lost-time claims. Internal and external stakeholders (*i.e.*, employees, employers, unions, and insurance providers and consultants) work together to seamlessly return a disabled employee to the labour market.

early intervention: management of a lost-time claim or probable claim from the time the disability is reported so as to ensure all reasonable action can be taken to facilitate an early and safe return to work. The goal of early intervention is to diminish the possibility of a disabled employee spending weeks or months off work.

employability: the essential skill sets and abilities that, if quantified over a given period of time, can be used to deem an employee either employable or unemployable. The most common skill sets are: punctuality, attendance, productivity, and ability to follow directions and learn new tasks.

experience rating: a program used by insurance companies and workers' compensation boards. The former uses the program to calculate risk, while the latter uses it to reward employers for practising good health and safety practices and for financially punishing employers who do not actively practise health and safety due diligence. The higher the costs that the insurance company or the workers' compensation board incurs on behalf of the employer — such as income replacement benefits — the more costly the premiums will be to the employer.

Functional Abilities Evaluation (FAE): an assessment that is used to quantify a disabled employee's physical abilities. A general FAE is a compilation of the employee's abilities. A specific FAE compares the employee's physical abilities to a given job. It will determine what aspects of the job are within the employee's abilities and which are not.

hard costs: the costs of having one or more employees off work due to disability (*i.e.*, overtime, replacement workers, insurance premiums, workers' compensation surcharges, training). *See also* **soft costs**.

hierarchy of objectives: a tool used to assist in the management of a lost-time claim. The objectives are: returning to the pre-disability job, returning to work with a comparable job, or returning to work with suitable work. By understanding what the objective is, the activities required to achieve that objective will become clearer. *See also* **suitable work**.

impairment: a loss or abnormality of a psychological, physiological or anatomical structure or function.

Independent Medical Evaluation (IME): an assessment usually performed by a physician or specialist who gives an educated opinion about various issues including diagnosis, treatment, prognosis and recommended treatment, if any.

job analysis: *See* **Physical Demands Analysis**.

lost-time claim: any disability that prevents an employee from performing and attending to the essential duties of his or her job when required to do so.

modified work: any work that will help an employee improve his or her ability to resume all or a portion of their regular job responsibilities. If the modified work program is not helping the disabled employee improve his or her physical abilities, stamina and endurance it is acting as a barrier to achieving a successful outcome.

non-compensable injury: any disability that occurs away from the workplace and is deemed to be a non-work-related injury and is therefore not considered to be a workers' compensation claim.

own occupation: a long-term disability insurance policy term. It is used to assist the insurance carrier in determining what, if any, income replacement benefits are payable. Income replacement benefits are usually payable for a two-year period if the disabled employee is unable to perform his or her pre-disability job responsibilities. After the two-year mark, benefits may be terminated if the insurance carrier determines that the disabled employee can perform other occupations based on his or her skills and abilities.

partially disabled: a term used to distinguish between a totally disabled employee and a partially disabled employee. It is assumed by most insurance providers, including workers' compensation boards, that if an employee is partially disabled that he or she is capable of performing some type of work soon after the onset of the disability.

Physical Demands Analysis (PDA): a detailed assessment of a specific job. It considers the essential responsibilities of the job, physical demands and possible workstation modifications to improve employee productivity and reduce body fatigue. A PDA is a valuable document to have when a specific FAE is being performed. The PDA will help the therapist quantify what aspects of the job the employee can and cannot perform.

Post-Offer Placement Evaluation: an assessment that may include a physical test and psychological tests including aptitude testing, interest testing and intelligence testing for the purposes of placing the employee in the most appropriate work environment. This assessment can also be used as a benchmark to compare an employee's abilities over time or after the onset of a disability.

psychometric testing: a battery of tests used to evaluate a disabled employee's psychological profile. *See also* **Psycho-Vocational Evaluation**.

Psycho-Vocational Evaluation: a battery of tests that includes tests administered by a vocational evaluator and an interview conducted by a psychologist. The testing provides information important to determining the employee's vocational profile and academic capabilities. The testing usually includes aptitude testing, intelligence testing, learning abilities, academic abilities such as spelling, reading, math, writing, grade levels and suggested job opportunities that are in keeping with the employee's abilities. The testing also takes into account the impact of the disability on the employee's life. The testing is quite valuable when considering whether an employee is a suitable candidate for formal retraining.

Second Injury Enhancement Fund (SIEF): a fund that compensates employers for workers' compensation claims that can be attributed to a previous claim. For example, an employee who sustains a back strain injury at employer A and some time later aggravates that back strain injury while employed with employer B, employer B would be entitled to receive compensation from the SIEF, having demonstrated to the compensation board that the claim would not have occurred if not for the original claim with employer A.

situational assessment: an assessment that assists the case manager in determining whether a disabled employee is employable. The assessment simulates a number of work settings that in turn can be used to evaluate an employee's ability to work. The employee performs a number of work tasks that have been confirmed as within his or her physical abilities and learning abilities several hours a day. All work activities are indirectly supervised. In most cases, the hours are increased as the employee demonstrates more ability. To appropriately assess the disabled employee, the assessment should be a minimum of four weeks to ensure the behaviours the employee demonstrates during the assessment are valid. The situational assessment is ideal for those individuals who have been out of the workforce for an extended period of time and will likely require a prolonged period to regain the strength, endurance and work behaviours required to be a productive employee again.

soft costs: costs that an employer will absorb when one or more disabled employees are absent from work yet cannot be easily quantified, for example, reduced productivity, morale and increased turnover. *See also* **hard costs**.

suitable work: a term used within the hierarchy of objectives. It is unique from the other objectives as it does not require the job to fully utilize the disabled employee's skills. This objective is commonly used when an employee is seriously disabled and unable to apply their skills to another comparable job due to the physical demands associated with that job or the employee's limited formal upgrading potential. *See also* **hierarchy of objectives**.

totally disabled: an employee that is physically and/or, emotionally and/or behaviourally unable to perform any work. An employee may be considered temporarily totally disabled if he or she is participating in medical treatment such as surgery.

Transferable Skills Analysis: an assessment that outlines the skills a disabled employee has acquired through work experience, both paid and volunteer; community activities, such as participation in sports, community groups; education and training including apprenticeship programs and skills upgrading like computer software and keyboarding. The report is used to help the case manager and disabled employee assess the appropriateness of alternate occupations. A transferable skills analysis is usually used once it has been determined that the disabled employee is unable to return to his or her pre-disability job or a comparable job with his or her current employer.

transitional work program: a program that assists a disabled employee's return to work performing a comparable or suitable job. The transition involves teaching the disabled employee new skills, usually on the job, thereby allowing him or her to attain the skills necessary to perform a physically suitable job. The transition period may occur over a six-month period.

undue hardship: a key term used in human rights legislation that, through precedent, defines to what extent employers are obligated to accommodate disabled employees to facilitate their return to work. In determining whether an employer has made a reasonable effort to accommodate a disabled employee, the Human Rights Commission will consider the cost of the accommodation, any impact the accommodation will have on the company's ability to remain competitive (*i.e.*, employee morale, safety considerations) and the reasonableness of the accommodation.

AN EMPLOYER'S GUIDE TO DISABILITY MANAGEMENT

vocational evaluation: a battery of tests administered by a vocational evaluator. The testing provides information important to determining the employee's vocational profile and academic capabilities. The testing will usually include: aptitude testing; intelligence testing; learning abilities; academic abilities such as spelling, reading, math, writing, grade levels; and suggested job opportunities that are in keeping with the employee's abilities, previous work experience, earning potential and labour market outlooks. The evaluation also considers the impact of the disability on the employee's life. In some cases it is difficult to match an employee's skills, physical abilities and pre-disability earnings with a new job based on a transferable skills analysis. The vocational evaluation will provide the case manager with more insight into the employee's abilities that in turn can be used to identify alternate career options.

vocational rehabilitation: the process of matching an employee's physical abilities, skills, knowledge, aptitudes, interests, training and experiences to an occupation.

work hardening: a work program commonly used for disabled employees who have been out of the workforce for a significant period of time (one year or more). The program allows the disabled individual to maximize his or her skills and abilities to the point that he or she is ready to re-enter the labour force. The work hardening program measures the employee's ability to work eight hours a day, five days a week, be punctual, follow instructions and demonstrate an acceptable level of productivity. This service is provided by an independent organization.

Index